D1034003

ASK A LAWYER
Landlord and Tenant

ALSO BY STEVEN D. STRAUSS

the *Ask a Lawyer* series

Divorce and Child Custody

Wills and Trusts

Debt and Bankruptcy

ASK A LAWYER

LANDLORD AND TENANT

Steven D. Strauss

W · W · NORTON & COMPANY

NEW YORK   LONDON

For information about permission to reproduce selections from this book, write to: Permissions, W. W. Norton & Company, Inc., 500 Fifth Avenue, New York, NY 10110.

The text of this book is composed in Berkeley Book, with the display set in Futura. Desktop composition by Chelsea Dippel. Manufacturing by the Haddon Craftsmen, Inc. Book design by Margaret Wagner.

Library of Congress Cataloging-in-Publication Data
Strauss, Steven D., 1958–
    Ask a lawyer. landlord and tenant / Steven D. Strauss.
        p.   cm.
    Includes index.
    ISBN 0-393-04585-4. — ISBN 0-393-31730-7 (pbk.)
    1. Landlord and tenant—United States—Popular works. I. Title.
KF590.S77 1998
346.7304'34—dc21   97-33617
                                                                CIP

W. W. Norton & Company, Inc. 500 Fifth Avenue, New York, N.Y. 10110
http://www.wwnorton.com

W. W. Norton & Company Ltd., 10 Coptic Street, London WC1A 1PU

1 2 3 4 5 6 7 8 9 0

This book is dedicated to my great bruhddies, Spencer and Larry, and to my wonderful sis, Robyn.

I would like to thank Seymour Fagan for everything he has taught me, legal and otherwise.

CONTENTS

INTRODUCTION: ABOUT THIS BOOK AND THE *ASK A LAWYER* SERIES

A person usually needs an attorney either to act as an advocate or to get advice. While there are many books on the market that endeavor to teach people how to be their own lawyer-advocate, this is not one of them. This book, and the *Ask a Lawyer* series, focuses upon the second function of an attorney—dispensing helpful, useful, and needed legal advice.

Few can afford to pay $250 to sit down with an attorney for an hour in order to get legal help. The *Ask a Lawyer* series is designed to give people the advice of an attorney at a fraction of the cost. Helping people understand the law and their rights, explaining which of several options may work best for them; giving insights, tips, and helpful hints; in short, giving readers the type of assistance they would expect if they sat down with an expensive lawyer, *is* the purpose of this book and this series.

Landlord and tenant law in particular is an area of the law that requires good, affordable legal help. As this book explains, there are many problems that can arise in this particular relationship; problems that can often cost either party a lot of money if not handled correctly. This book will help you figure out how best to resolve such issues. How do you handle a landlord who refuses to return a security deposit? What do you do with a tenant who continually fails to pay rent on time? How should an eviction be handled? Read on.

This book will sensibly walk you through landlord and tenant rights and responsibilities, caution you about possible pitfalls, explain in simple terms important aspects of the law, and guide you toward a sensible solution to your particular problem. It is organized to make this often complicated area of the law quite easy to understand. Each chapter has its own table of contents, so that once you turn to a chapter of interest to you, you can quickly find the specific area with which you need help. If, for example, you have a question about who should fix a leaky faucet, flip to Chapter 14, "The Duty to Provide a Habitable Home and Repair the Premises," and look under "The duty to repair necessities." Each chapter ends with "The Important Legal Concepts to Remember" so that you leave the topic understanding exactly what it is you need to know.

Appendix A lists many common landlord and tenant questions, along with sensible, simple answers. Any **boldface** word in this book can be found in the glossary, Appendix B.

Unlike many other areas of the law, resolving landlord-tenant disputes usually does not require the assistance of an attorney. Since this book easily explains each side's rights and duties, the need for a lawyer to resolve a dispute is eliminated. No book of this type can come with a guarantee, and no book can substitute for the advice of an attorney familiar with your particular problems and issues. However, absent many hours with high-priced legal counsel, this book is just about the next best thing.

BEFORE YOU
RENT

A NOTE TO LANDLORDS
AND TENANTS

The landlord-tenant relationship
Landlord-tenant law in general

Compare this scenario:

Ari had lived in a home owned by Raphael for three years.
Ari had always been a good tenant and Raphael a good landlord. However, when the house's fence fell down after a big
storm, Raphael refused to fix it. He claimed that Ari's toma-
to vines, which had climbed the fence for years, were the
cause. Raphael therefore claimed it was Ari's responsibility to
fix it. Ari believed that since Raphael was the landlord, he
should fix it.

Tempers flared, and neither party would budge. Ari
stopped paying rent. Raphael threatened to evict him. In
the end, Ari *was* evicted for his failure to pay rent. However, in the meantime, Raphael fell behind on his mortgage due
to the lack of rent, and the fence was never fixed by the time
the bank foreclosed on the house.

with this scenario:

After the fence fell down and the yelling had subsided,
Raphael realized that he needed to solve this problem lest

he be faced with a much larger one. He sat down with Ari one day over a cup of coffee and said, "Listen, Ari, I need your rent and you need a place to live. If I buy the lumber, would you be willing to put up a new fence?" Ari knew that an eviction would make finding a new home very difficult. "Sure," he said. "That's a fair compromise."

THE LANDLORD-TENANT RELATIONSHIP. Before you arm yourself with laws, statutes, and other ammunition to hurl at your **landlord** or **tenant**, it is important to understand a *nonlegal* concept: the landlord-tenant relationship is, first of all, a relationship. Like all relationships, it can be positive or negative. It can be friendly or adversarial. It can be mutually beneficial or mutually detrimental. It is up to the parties in the relationship to determine the quality of that relationship.

Yes, knowing your rights will undoubtedly help to solve a problem. Yet no knowledge of the law can be more effective than this basic rule of landlord-tenant relationships: *Nothing beats a good working relationship with your landlord or tenant.* A friendly, personal call by a landlord to a tenant whose **rent** is tardy is often more effective than a hostile threat of **eviction** backed by rules and statutes.

So, this is your first tip: try to cultivate a positive, working relationship with your counterpart in this relationship. Be fair and responsible. You will find that it will be much easier to get what you want if that person likes and trusts you than if he dislikes and resents you. In that sense, the landlord-tenant dance is just like any other—work together or someone will step on the other's feet.

LANDLORD-TENANT LAW IN GENERAL. Try as you might to get along with your dance partner, it is not always possible. Some people are simply too mean or too stupid or too irresponsible or too bureaucratic to work with. When faced with people or institutions like these, it is best to come armed instead of friendly.

In the context of landlord-tenant law, that means knowing your legal rights and the other party's legal responsibilities. A tenant who knows that she is not normally legally responsible for a fallen fence will not be bamboozled so easily. A landlord who knows that he is not normally legally responsible for a tenant-created problem will not be so quick to open his wallet. So, this is your second tip: know your rights.

Tenancy is the term used for the period of time that a tenant rents a unit from a landlord. A tenancy can last any length—a week, a month, a year, or more. A tenancy can be created in writing or by verbal agreement. No matter the type of arrangement, any rental creates a tenancy. What is important to understand is that the creation of a tenancy simultaneously and automatically creates rights and duties on both sides.

And just what are those rights? Prior to the 1960s, landlords held all the cards in the legal deck. Tenants had very few rights, and landlords had many. Although it is well known that the consumer rights movement of the 1970s drastically changed the rights of consumers, what is less well known is that it had an equal, if not greater, effect on landlord-tenant law.

Whereas landlords in previous eras could collect rent without having to provide little more than a roof in return, today they are obligated by law to provide safe, clean, and **habitable** dwellings. Landlords are now prevented from **discriminating** in housing, **rent control** has taken effect in many communities, and landlords in most **jurisdictions** are forbidden from raising rent, shutting off utilities, or evicting a tenant in retaliation for some minor dispute.

Yet, while the scale has definitely tilted in favor of the tenant, landlords are not without protections. A landlord is, after all, still the owner of the property and law itself was created to protect property rights. If rent is late or a tenant becomes a problem, expeditious evictions are available. If a tenant harms the property, the **lease** can be terminated. If a tenant uses the unit to break the law, a landlord can immediately end any agreement.

Landlords and tenants are mutually dependent upon one another. Landlords depend upon their tenants for rent, and tenants need landlords for a place to live. So, although everyone is now legally armed with rights, responsibilities, and **remedies**, remember that it takes two to tango.

The Important Legal Concept to Remember: It is a lot easier to be friendly to your landlord or tenant if you know your rights. If kindness fails to solve a problem, the law will.

BEFORE THE TENANT MOVES IN

What the tenant should look for
How to find the right tenant
Discrimination in housing

Before a lease is ever signed, before the cat is deemed acceptable, before the fence ever falls down, the wary landlord and the prospective tenant first must meet. Renting an apartment or house from or to someone you do not know is a risky venture. A landlord needs proof that the tenant is responsible. A tenant needs proof that the unit is habitable.

WHAT THE TENANT SHOULD LOOK FOR. Any tenant wanting to rent space from a landlord needs to inspect the premises thoroughly before any agreement is reached. The first thing to do is to check out the neighborhood and speak with some neighbors. It would be especially helpful if you could speak with other people who rent from the same landlord.

Although she liked the apartment her potential landlord, Paul, had shown her, Anne decided to speak with some neighbors before signing the year-long lease. She was glad she did. It turned out that Paul had a reputation for being difficult, and rarely fixed problems in a timely manner. Anne found a similar apartment with a good landlord instead.

Besides the neighborhood and the neighbors, be sure to check out thoroughly the condition of the unit too. This is especially important in order to discover any defects on the premises. If, for example, the unit has a window pane that is broken, it would behoove the prospective tenant to bring it to the landlord's attention so that the landlord does not later try to blame the new tenant for the old problem.

If the unit you are looking at has some of the problems listed below, either the landlord should fix them first or you should not rent the space. As explained in Chapter 6, implied in *every* **rental agreement** is something called the **implied warranty of habitability**. That warranty means that every residential landlord is obliged to provide every tenant with a dwelling that is livable. If the unit lacks basic necessities *before* a tenant ever moves in, make no mistake about it, it certainly will not have them later, no matter what promises are made.

- *Plumbing:* Be on the lookout for leaky faucets, water around the base of the toilet, drains that don't drain, and rusty-colored water. Make sure that the hot water works.
- *Kitchen:* Does the stove work? Is the sink clean? Does the refrigerator door close? Try sticking a dollar bill in the door; the harder it is to pull out, the better.
- *Structure:* Is the unit weatherproof? Look for water stains and excessive caulking near windows, and stains on the ceiling and down the walls. Be sure too that any linoleum floors are not curling, since **liability** could be a problem if someone trips.
- *Heat and air:* While laws mandate that a rental unit must have adequate heat, air-conditioning is not usually required by statute.
- *Fire safety:* Most cities require smoke detectors to be installed

in rental units. Stairways, hallways, and storage areas should be free of combustible materials.

After the inspection is complete and the landlord wants to rent to you, be sure to list on the rental agreement all problems that you found with the rental. Moreover, make sure to get in writing any promises the landlord makes, such as assurances that he will fix a leaky faucet or repaint before you move in. That way, there will be no misunderstandings.

HOW TO FIND THE RIGHT TENANT. Needless to say, finding the right tenant is critical to the success of a landlord's business. When looking for a tenant, a landlord needs to be quite careful.

Of course, he must find a tenant with a good rental and credit history—that is a given. Equally important, though, legally speaking, are the many laws that apply to landlords when they are looking for tenants. Probably the most important laws to know about are antidiscrimination statutes, which dictate that a landlord cannot discriminate when renting out his property. When advertising for a prospective tenant, the smart landlord should not mention race, sex, age, national origin, or religion. Discrimination in rental housing is forbidden and such ads can be misconstrued (see below).

Once a landlord has located some prospective tenants, he should have them fill out a rental application and list their rental history, credit history, and references. He must make sure to call the references, including previous landlords. What is necessary to know is whether a possible tenant has a history of paying rent on time, if he has ever been evicted, and whether he caused problems previously. It is also a good idea to verify the employment and income of any prospective tenant.

It is also wise to run a credit check on the possible tenant. Charging the tenant a nominal **fee** (say, twenty-five dollars) for the time and expense of running the credit check is legal in most states, and advisable. If you use the report to deny an application, federal law mandates that you notify the applicant and tell him the name and address of the credit agency upon which your decision was based.

Many landlords choose not to interview or rent to potential tenants who have pets. While perfectly legal and understandable, they may want to reconsider that position. Pet owners tend to be more stable and better occupants than tenants without pets. Many will pay higher rents and large **deposits** just to have a place where they can have a pet. They also are more reluctant to leave since finding a new rental that accepts a pet is often difficult. The upshot is that renting to a pet owner means a landlord may get a tenant who will pay more, leave a larger deposit, and probably will not leave too quickly. Not a bad deal.

DISCRIMINATION IN HOUSING. If you are faced with two equally qualified tenants, it is legal to pick one over another for no other reason than that you liked one better; there is nothing discriminatory about that. However, if you have a pattern of not choosing African-Americans, women, or other minorities, you leave yourself open to an expensive discrimination lawsuit, even if you never actually intended to discriminate against anyone.

Regardless of whether you are the manager of a one-hundred-unit apartment complex or the owner of a small duplex, federal antidiscrimination laws apply to you, as may several state and local ordinances. The federal Civil Rights Act and Fair Housing Act prohibit landlords from discriminating on the basis of race, ethnic background, national origin, religion, and sex. It is also illegal to discriminate against families with children. The Americans with Disabilities Act (ADA) effectively prohibits discrimination against someone with a disability.

Not only are landlords forbidden from denying a tenant a unit because of her race, religion, or sex, but it is also illegal to provide inferior housing, or to state that a unit is unavailable when that is not so. In essence, a landlord cannot reject a prospective tenant, or allegedly discriminate against her in any way, for any reason other than "legitimate and valid business reasons." Whereas denying a woman a unit because you do not like her religion is flatly illegal, denying her the place because she has a poor credit history is not. The bottom line: a landlord must have a valid business reason for any potentially discriminatory act.

The only time a landlord can legally discriminate against a family with children (assuming, of course, that the unit is large enough to accommodate such a family) is if the complex is designated "seniors only." A landlord does not, however, have to rent a two-bedroom place to a qualified applicant who has five children. Reasonable occupancy standards are expected and permissible.

The only time discrimination is legally permissible is when the unit is "owner-occupied"; that is, if the owner and the tenant will be sharing a house, for example, or otherwise may be sharing kitchen and bathroom facilities. In that case, antidiscrimination laws do not apply since such arrangements are not considered a business venture, and these antidiscrimination laws apply only to businesses.

Even if he is not discriminating, a landlord should be equally concerned with the *appearance* of discrimination. If you have a complex occupied only by whites, for example, then you may appear to be discriminating, even if you are not. The key to minimizing that risk is to set up some objective, legitimate business criteria when looking for new tenants and to stick to them. What you must do is to look *consistently* for things such as two positive references, stable employment, and a good credit history. Treat people equally and use the same criteria in every case. It may even be wise to write down your criteria and keep it on file. Above all, *be consistent, and document your reasons for denying someone a unit.*

If you do discriminate, the affected person can **sue** in state or federal court, or can file an administrative complaint with the Department of Housing and Urban Development (HUD). If you are found to have violated federal antidiscrimination housing laws, the ramifications can be severe. Authorities can order you to rent the unit to the person discriminated against, as well as force you to pay **damages** (i.e., money). Such money damages may not only include the out-of-pocket expenses of the **plaintiff**, but also money for pain, suffering, humiliation, and attorney's fees. Punitive damages, if applicable, can bankrupt a person.

The Important Legal Concept to Remember: Both landlords and tenants need to do their homework and check each other out before any agreements are signed. Landlords must treat all prospective tenants equally.

A CRASH COURSE IN LEASES AND RENTAL AGREEMENTS

Month-to-month agreements

Leases

Understanding written leases and written rental agreements

Written month-to-month rental agreements are usually best for landlords

Why fixed-term leases are best for tenants

There are two types of rental arrangements that a landlord and tenant can enter into: periodic tenancies and **fixed-term agreements**. A fixed-term agreement is popularly known as a **lease**. The more common name for a periodic tenancy is a **month-to-month agreement**.

MONTH-TO-MONTH AGREEMENTS. The first thing to understand about a periodic tenancy is that the period can be any length of time; a month is only the most common (and, therefore, is used most often in this book). Landlords and tenants can agree to any length of time; it all depends upon how often rent is due. If rent is due once a month, then it is a month-to-month agreement. If it is due every week, then it is a weekly agreement. The period corresponds to the frequency of rent payments.

The length of time of the period is critical. The second, and most important, thing to know about periodic tenancies is that the agreement can change on *very short notice*; again, depending upon how often rent is due.

Claire entered into a month-to-month agreement with her landlord, Howard. Rent was set at $750 per month. After living in the unit for only two months, Howard gave Claire thirty days' notice of a rent increase. The new amount of rent was to be $1,500 a month. Claire's only two choices were either to pay the grossly inflated increase or to move.

Almost any change is permissible with a periodic tenancy, as long as proper **notice** has been given. Rent can be raised. The agreement can be **terminated**. A tenant can be told that a pet will no longer be welcome. Again, the amount of notice required to change the terms of the deal corresponds directly to how often rent is due. If rent is due every thirty days, then the amount of time required to change the terms of the agreement is also thirty days. If rent is due weekly, then the agreement could be terminated on seven days' notice. So, the important thing to know about month-to-month agreements is that *thirty days is all that is required to change the agreement.*

The agreement, while month-to-month, can actually *last* any length of time—a month or five years. It depends on what the parties want. As long as a tenant pays rent on time and cares for the unit, and as long as a landlord lives up to his duties, there is nothing stopping them from keeping the agreement going as long as they want to.

Month-to-month agreements can be made either verbally or in writing; there is no legal requirement that the arrangement has to be in writing, although it is a very good idea (see below). Changes in the terms of the agreement also do not have to be in writing. A landlord can give a tenant thirty days' notice to vacate over the phone.

LEASES. The second type of agreement that landlords and tenants can enter into is called a fixed-term agreement, commonly known as a lease. A lease is different from a month-to-month agreement in that it fixes all terms of the agreement for a specific period of time, typically, but not necessarily, one year. Whereas a monthly rental arrangement can change on thirty days' notice, *no changes* can occur in the terms of the lease while the lease is in effect. Rent cannot be raised. A landlord cannot give notice and force a tenant to move on thirty days' notice. It is because the contract does lock in the terms of the agreement for a fixed period of time that a lease is known as a fixed-term agreement.

And just as the landlord is obliged to allow the tenant to stay in the unit for a year, the tenant is obliged to pay rent for the full year. If a tenant has a year-long lease and moves out after nine months, he is legally obliged to pay the remaining three months' rent, whether or not he is living in the dwelling. A lease is a year-long **contract** obligating both sides.

Another important thing to realize about a lease is that, unlike a month-to-month agreement, it ends *automatically*. No notice needs to be given to terminate a lease. When the lease term ends, that is it. The tenant is supposed to move out that day, unless the lease has been renewed.

Whereas a month-to-month arrangement can be made either verbally or in writing, a lease *must* be in writing due to something called the statute of frauds. That statute mandates that certain types of contracts must be in writing to be valid. Under the statute of frauds, agreements that last a year or more, and that pertain to land and real estate, like leases, are required to be in writing to have any legal effect. If they are not, it is as if no agreement was ever made. An oral lease that purports to last longer than a year is **void**.

UNDERSTANDING WRITTEN LEASES AND WRITTEN RENTAL AGREEMENTS. As indicated, when a landlord and a tenant enter into a month-to-month agreement, that agreement can be either verbal or written. Verbal monthly agreements are a very bad idea for everyone.

A landlord can promise a tenant the moon, but if it is not in writing, it will be very difficult to get those promises enforced. A tenant can promise to take care of the yard in return for a lower monthly rental payment, but if it is not in writing, there is no way to prove the agreement. Moreover, people may have different perceptions about what was agreed to. Memories fade over time. There are simply too many areas for disagreement when an oral contract is entered into. So, it is an altogether better idea to get any rental arrangement in writing.

When a month-to-month arrangement is memorialized in writing, it is called a rental agreement. When a fixed-term agreement is memorialized in writing, it is called a lease. (Thus, a lease really has two meanings: it is both the *term* for the type of agreement the landlord and tenant have and also the *name* of that agreement.)

A written rental agreement looks very much like a written lease. Both state who the parties to the agreement are and where the unit is located, and list the amount of rent. Both likely contain many boilerplate legal provisions that tend to favor the landlord. Not knowing the difference however, can have severe ramifications.

Upon graduation from college, Bill found an apartment that he loved for $1,000 a month and signed what he thought was a month-to-month rental agreement. When he was let go from his new job two months later, he gave thirty days' notice and intended to move home with his parents for a while. His landlord informed him that he had signed a lease and was responsible for the entire year of rent. Bill ignored him. Bill's landlord sued Bill for $10,000 ($1,000 x 10 months) and won.

While many such written rental contracts indicate clearly whether it is a yearly lease or a monthly rental agreement, some do not. A landlord has no problem distinguishing a lease from a rental agreement; he or she uses them all the time. How can a tenant tell them apart? The important thing to look for is a provision that *allows the agreement to be terminated, or rent to be raised, on thirty days' notice.* Such a clause means that the agreement is a month-to-month tenancy and not a fixed-term lease.

Neither leases nor rental agreements can legally include provisions that attempt to circumvent rental laws. Tenants have the right to habitable dwellings, to **privacy**, to use the place in **quiet enjoyment**, to minimum-notice requirements if they are being sued, and to a speedy return of deposits. Any agreement containing clauses that attempt to force tenants to **waive** (forgo) these rights is flatly illegal and unenforceable.

Either agreement can be intimidating; they are seemingly written in stone. But the truth is that they are changed all the time. Any written rental arrangement, be it a lease or a rental agreement, is a contract. Like any contract, both sides must agree to it. If a landlord wants to add an extra provision and both sides agree, then that provision can be added. If a tenant wants to delete a questionable clause and the landlord agrees, then it can be crossed out, and the change initialed and dated. Neither tenant nor landlord should ever sign an agreement that he does not agree with. That is why it is called an agreement.

Tenants especially may think that changing a lease or a rental agreement offered by a prospective landlord is practically impossible, but it is not usually as difficult as they may think. Landlords are in the business of renting their property. Unrented property is lost money. By the time a tenant is reading and ready to sign a rental agreement, his potential landlord has already concluded that he is the best available prospect. The landlord wants to rent to this tenant. Believe it or not, that tenant is in the power position.

Norman wanted Robyn to move into his vacant unit. Robyn was interested, but really wanted to bring her cat along, and Norman normally did not allow animals in the apartment.

Robyn knew that the space had been empty for a while, and she also knew that her previous landlord would give her a great referral. She insisted that she be allowed to bring her cat. Since Norman really wanted Robyn as a tenant, he agreed to the cat, changed the lease, and had Robyn put down an extra $200 cleaning deposit.

WRITTEN MONTH-TO-MONTH RENTAL AGREEMENTS ARE USUALLY BEST FOR LANDLORDS. Written monthly rental agreements are best for the tenant who does not plan to stay in the unit too long because the arrangement allows him to move on little notice. They are bad for the tenant who wants some security.

While they are sometimes good for tenants, written monthly rental agreements are often better for landlords, as these agreements keep power in a landlord's hands. First of all, it is the landlord's form. The landlord either buys the form (written by attorneys for landlords) from a stationery store or legal bookstore, or has his attorney draft it, or drafts it himself. In any case, the agreement protects the landlord at the expense of the tenant.

Even more important, these agreements permit changes on short notice—that is the very nature of a month-to-month agreement. This fact almost always helps a landlord. If a tenant becomes a problem, he can be out upon thirty days' notice. If a variable-rate interest mortgage on the unit suddenly increases, rents can be raised on thirty days' notice. This simply is not true with a lease. Leases lock everyone into the agreement for the entire term of the agreement. Month-to-month agreements let landlords make changes quickly if needed, and that is a great advantage.

Really, from the landlord's point of view, the only downside to using a monthly rental agreement is that it provides less security. Knowing that a house will be rented for a year is seemingly a great comfort. *Seemingly.* Leases are broken all the time. Unpaid rents are a fact. Security may be a myth. In most cases, the flexibility of a shorter-term agreement usually outweighs any perceived security of a lease.

WHY FIXED-TERM LEASES ARE BEST FOR TENANTS. Whereas a written monthly rental agreement favors the landlord, a fixed-term lease is often in the best interests of a tenant. First of all, a lease does give a tenant security. She knows that unless she gives the landlord **good cause** to evict her (such as ruining the apartment or not paying rent), she will have a place to live until the term expires. She also knows that her rent will not go up during that period.

Maybe best of all from the tenant's perspective is that she can probably break the lease without repercussion, if need be. This gives her the security of a lease with the flexibility of a monthly rental agreement. That is a hard combination to beat.

Under normal circumstances, a tenant is obliged to pay the entire year's worth of rent, even if she does not stay in the unit the entire time. That is the price one pays for the security that comes with a lease. If a tenant leaves with six months remaining on her lease, she is technically obliged to pay those six months of rent, with one very important caveat.

That is this: under contract law, landlords have a **duty** to try to rerent the unit as soon as is feasible. This is called **mitigating** one's damages. A landlord must take reasonable steps to reduce any damage he may suffer as a result of a tenant's breach of the lease. Renting the unit again in a reasonable amount of time to a qualified tenant would be a landlord's mitigation. In the case of the tenant who leaves with six months left on the lease, if a landlord rented the place again in three months, then his actual monetary loss would only be the three months that the house was vacant. The tenant who moved early would be obliged to pay her landlord only for those three months.

Even more problematic for the landlord is that collecting that lost money is often difficult and not worth the time and expense it would take.

Alice signed a year-long lease with Stephen. She was to pay $500 a month in rent. Six months into the term, Alice was offered a better job in a different city and moved out. It took Stephen three months to rent the place again. Although Alice was legally obligated to pay Stephen $1,500 ($500 x the 3 months that the place was vacant), Stephen knew in reality that he would never see that money. Alice didn't live there anymore. Stephen did not even know where to find her. Alice never paid the money and Stephen never even asked for it.

Leases are broken—that's a fact—and most often by tenants. Tenants really have little to lose by breaking a lease. A sad but true fact is that tenants usually do not have much money. People without many assets are known to lawyers as "empty pockets." No lawyer wants to sue an empty pocket. Accordingly, a landlord may not even go to the effort to sue over a broken lease, and even if he does, he may have a hard time collecting on any **judgment** he may eventually get.

Thus, not only is the landlord legally obliged to mitigate his losses when a tenant breaks a lease and moves early, but suing the tenant is usually not worth the landlord's effort. Since most landlords know this, a tenant can usually break a lease without consequence, if need be.

Accordingly, *a tenant should almost always get a lease if at all possible.* It obligates the landlord, prevents him from raising rent, and stops him from terminating the agreement unless good cause exists. A lease gives a tenant security without, in reality, any of the anchors.

The Important Legal Concept to Remember: Rental agreements vary greatly. Landlords should usually try to get their tenants to enter into written rental agreements, and tenants should almost always try to get a lease.

COMMON LEASE AND RENTAL AGREEMENT PROVISIONS

▰▰▰

Common provisions

Provisions to be wary of if you are a tenant

Which provisions landlords should be most concerned with

COMMON PROVISIONS. The following are the ten most important sections in any lease or rental agreement. As a lease or rental agreement can be changed before it is signed, if any corresponding provision in your agreement is vague or unclear, make sure to clarify it. If and when a dispute arises, it will be this agreement that everyone will look to—judges especially—when determining who did wrong to whom.

1. *Identification of the parties and limits on occupancy:* The agreement must name the landlord and the tenants. A tenant who anticipates that his girlfriend may be moving in within two months should get her name on the agreement at the beginning of the term to avoid any confusion or later cause for eviction. If the agreement states that the unit is limited to four people, then the unit is limited to four people.

2. *Rent:* The agreement should clearly spell out when, where, and how much rent is due. It should also indicate if there is a grace period and any penalty for late payment of rent.

3. *Term:* Is this a month-to-month tenancy or a lease? Again, leases end automatically at the end of the term. Month-to-month tenancies normally end upon thirty days' notice. If the document allows modifications on thirty days' notice, it is a month-to-month rental agreement.

4. *Deposits:* The deposit clause should clarify how much deposit is required and to what it will be applied. The custom is to use the deposit for cleaning, unpaid rent, and damage above and beyond normal **wear and tear**. **Last month's rent** may be included in the **security deposit**, as long as it is clear that that is the case. That money can thereafter be used only to pay the last month of rent. The amount of a security deposit is often limited by state law; the equivalent of two months' rent is common. (For more information, see Chapter 10, "Security Deposits and Last Month's Rent.")

5. *Pets:* It is the landlord's right to allow or not to allow pets. If a tenant plans on bringing in a pet, even something as innocuous as a guinea pig, it is best to get the landlord's permission, again to avoid confusion or cause for eviction. A landlord cannot legally prohibit an animal that is used to assist someone who is blind, deaf, or disabled.

6. *Subletting and assignments:* **Subletting** is when the renter allows someone else to move into the space and pay the rent, but remains liable under the lease. An **assignment** takes the original tenant out of the agreement altogether; the new person takes over all obligations under the contract. Assignments and sublets may or may not be allowed under the agreement, but they usually are as long as the landlord first approves of the proposed change. The landlord cannot unreasonably withhold approval. (See Chapter 18, "Getting Out of a Lease Early.")

7. *Utilities:* The agreement should specify which utility bills are part of the rent and which are the additional responsibility of the tenant. Landlords usually pay for garbage, and tenants usually pay for phone, gas, and electric.

8. *Attorney fees and costs:* This clause states that the loser of any lawsuit must pay the legal fees and costs of the winner. As landlords win most eviction lawsuits, this clause effectively shifts the legal cost of eviction from the landlord to the tenant. This section *is* legal, and if a tenant is evicted under an agreement with such a provision, the tenant will be liable for all of the landlord's legal costs.

9. *Entire agreement:* This clause states that the document is the entire agreement between the parties, and that any previous oral promises are superseded by this contract. If your landlord or tenant made any promises to you earlier, you had better include them in this document, as they will be of *no effect* once the agreement is signed.

10. *Inspection notes:* A smart tenant will closely inspect the premises prior to signing the agreement and will note all defects.

PROVISIONS TO BE WARY OF IF YOU ARE A TENANT. Since leases and rental agreements are written by or for landlords, more often than not they favor the landlord. This is not to say that all landlords are unscrupulous; most certainly are not. Rather, it is a word of caution to the overzealous landlord and the too-trusting tenant—there are provisions in some rental agreements that are illegal and that may either harm the tenant or render the agreement altogether void. The most onerous are the following:

- *Waiver of the tenant's right to privacy:* This sort of clause endeavors to allow the landlord to enter the unit on no notice and without the tenant's permission. Since every residential rental agreement has implicit in it a tenant's right to privacy (called the **implied covenant of quiet enjoyment**), this clause is illegal and unenforceable.
- *No liability for damages or injuries:* This clause attempts to protect the landlord from having to pay money if the tenant

is injured due to the landlord's negligent maintenance or upkeep of the property. Such provisions are also illegal and unenforceable.

- *Waiver of legal rights:* A **waiver** is a voluntary relinquishment of a known right. Although a contract may attempt to have the tenant waive certain rights, some rights are simply nonwaivable, no matter what the contract says. For instance, although the right to a jury trial for an eviction proceeding is guaranteed by many states, some rental contracts endeavor to have the tenant waive this right. Similarly, clauses that allow the landlord to evict the tenant without proper notice, that force the tenant to waive the right to appeal a court decision in an eviction action, that waive refunds of security deposits, or that waive applicable rent control ordinances are blatantly illegal and unenforceable.

- *Repairs:* Landlords are almost universally obligated to make major repairs. This is due to another rule implied in every residential agreement, called the implied warranty of habitability. This warranty means that it is up to the landlord to ensure that the dwelling is livable and that it is his responsibility if it is not. A lease provision that attempts to circumvent this rule is most likely void.

Tenants faced with agreements that contain provisions such as these have two choices: fight or do nothing. Of the two, doing nothing is, surprisingly, probably preferable. Think about it. Getting into a dispute with a landlord before he is even your landlord is a good way to ensure that he will never be your landlord. If you simply say nothing, comfortable in the knowledge that illegal provisions are void and unenforceable, then you will get the place *and* have a lease without the questionable provisions.

Richard's landlord, Frederick, had a lease that stated that Frederick would not be responsible if Richard were ever injured due to Frederick's negligence. Richard later sued Frederick after he was scalded by a faulty water heater that Frederick was well aware of. Richard won the lawsuit, and the questionable lease provision was completely ignored by the judge.

Remember, such provisions are unenforceable—no judge will make you pay for major repairs not of your creation, no matter what the contract says.

Aside from these illegal provisions, there are other provisions that, while legal, are at least negotiable. For instance, a prohibition against subletting or assignment without the landlord's permission is certainly negotiable. A pet restriction is often worth discussing. Whereas reasonable late charges for tardy rent are permissible, unreasonable penalties (say, 10 percent of the rent) are not and should be changed.

WHICH PROVISIONS LANDLORDS SHOULD BE MOST CON-CERNED WITH. There are two aspects of lease and rental agreements that landlords need to be concerned about. The first are the provisions listed above, which are clearly illegal. Landlords need to be careful not to load up their contracts with too many illegal or questionable provisions. A principal of contract law is that some contracts are interpreted *against* the maker. That is, a court looking at a rental agreement drawn up by a landlord may likely analyze that contract in a light that favors the tenant. An agreement that contains too many questionable clauses may be disregarded in its entirety.

Even if a contract does not contain any illegal sections, the cautious landlord will want to protect his interests by making certain aspects of the agreement nonnegotiable:

• *Limits on occupancy and use:* You certainly do not want your tenants inviting their in-laws and cousins to move in after the agreement has been signed. Note, however, that it is normally perfectly legal for a tenant to bring in a spouse and children later without a landlord's consent. Also, a residential unit should be limited to that purpose only. While local zoning laws may prohibit businesses from being run out of the unit, it is a good idea to limit use specifically (if that is your desire).

· *Rent:* For the most part, the amount of rent, when and where it is due, charges for late rent, and bounced-check charges should not be subject to negotiation.

· *Prohibition against assignment and subletting:* This clause normally prevents the tenant from replacing herself in the middle of the term with another tenant whom you do not know and may not approve of. While an outright ban on sublets may be illegal in your area, a clause requiring your express written consent of the new person is not, as long as that consent is not unreasonably withheld.

· *Condition, alteration, and damage to the premises:* Sometimes appearing in separate clauses, this section limits the landlord's liability for damage to the unit caused by the tenant. A landlord is responsible for repairing items that break due to normal wear and tear (such as a leaky faucet or an old refrigerator that finally dies), and the tenant is responsible for damages that he or his guests create. Make sure this is spelled out clearly in the agreement. Should he so choose, a landlord can restrict alterations to the unit, such as building bookcases or painting.

Here is one more thing to consider: as indicated, most standard agreements permit the winner of any lawsuit to collect attorney fees and court costs from the loser. Landlords should think carefully about whether they really want this clause in their agreement. The first problem with this is that a landlord might end up paying a tenant's legal expenses. And if that were not bad enough, the clause may actually encourage a tenant to fight, given the possibility that she will be reimbursed should she win.

The Important Legal Concept to Remember: Like any contract, a rental agreement is completely negotiable. Try to
get as many helpful clauses inserted into the contract as
possible. Landlords should be especially conscious not to
add in too many questionable clauses that would make the
agreement unenforceable.

II

TENANT RIGHTS, DUTIES, AND SOLUTIONS

THE TENANT'S RIGHT TO POSSESSION

Understanding the right of possession
When the landlord can enter
Fixtures

When a landlord rents property to a tenant, certain rights and responsibilities come into effect as a matter of law. What is important to realize is that these rights are *automatic*. They exist *whether or not they are mentioned in the agreement* and are created whenever a tenant moves into a unit. The first of these rights is called the right to possession.

UNDERSTANDING THE RIGHT OF POSSESSION. A rental agreement is a contract. As with any contract, both sides make promises. The tenant promises to take care of the unit and to pay the rent in full and on time. The landlord promises to let the tenant live in the property to the exclusion of everyone else. Although the landlord owns the dwelling, by entering into the rental contract with the tenant, he is foregoing his right to possess the property in lieu of the rent money received.

Hannah lived in a lovely home for many years. While she lived there, she cultivated a beautiful garden in the backyard. When she inherited some money, Hannah decided to buy a bigger place and rent out her house. She found what she thought to be the perfect tenant in Jenny, and leased it to her for a year. After Hannah moved out, she told Jenny that she would be coming back to the house once a month to clip some flowers from the garden. Jenny correctly informed Hannah that the house was now hers and that Hannah was not welcome.

The reason why a landlord cannot enter is because once a tenancy is created, so is the right to exclusive possession. Both a month-to-month tenancy and a lease give the tenant the exclusive right to control the premises.

This right to exclusive possession extends to the entire property.

Although Hannah had been out of the house for six months, she never emptied the garage, despite Jenny's repeated requests for her to do so. Finally, Jenny sued Hannah in small claims court, and the judge awarded Jenny $500 as compensation for not having use of the garage attached to the house she rented.

Had she wanted to, Jenny could have voided the lease, moved out, and not paid another penny in rent. This is due to a concept known as **constructive eviction**. If a landlord takes possession of all or even part of the premises without permission, the tenant can cancel the lease and leave. (See Chapter 18, "Getting Out of a Lease Early.")

Thus, the right to possession means that once the unit has been rented to the tenant, it is hers to possess, to the exclusion of everyone, including the landlord. However, some landlords do not know the law. They think that because they own the premises, they still have the right to enter the unit whenever they want to. This is just not so. Once the landlord delivers the unit to the tenant, the tenant has the sole right to possession. After the tenant moves in, her home is her castle.

This point should be underscored. Even though the landlord may own the property, even though the landlord pays the taxes and is responsible for maintenance, and even though the landlord has a right to exclusive control of the property *before* it is rented, once occupied, it is the tenant who has the right to exclusive control of the property.

WHEN THE LANDLORD CAN ENTER. This right to exclusive control is not absolute, however. There are times when the landlord needs to enter the unit, even if the tenant may not want him to. In the situations listed below, landlords retain the right to enter the unit:

- *Showing the unit to prospective tenants:* If the landlord will soon be renting the unit to a new tenant, he has the right to show it to prospective tenants. Again, he can do so even if the tenant in possession does not want to let him in.
- *Repairs:* If repairs to the unit are needed, the landlord can enter in order to make those repairs.
- *Court order:* If a tenant has been evicted yet still refuses to move out, a landlord has the right to enter, although he should consider bringing the sheriff or a police officer along.
- *Emergencies:* Should an actual emergency, such as a fire or a medical crisis, warrant it, a landlord may immediately come into the unit without any notice whatsoever. A trumped up excuse, such as "I thought I heard the water running for too long," will not do; it must be a real emergency.

Absent an emergency (when he can enter the unit immediately), a landlord is required to give his tenant "reasonable" notice of his intent to enter. In most cases, twenty-four to forty-eight hours is considered reasonable. After proper notice has been given, the landlord should enter only during normal business hours. If the landlord does not give proper notice, ironically enough, he will be considered a **trespasser** on his own land.

FIXTURES. Once a tenant has exclusive control of the unit, he may want to improve the property by building a bookcase or a deck, for example, or by painting a room. Normally, the landlord's permission is needed before such improvements can be made, since even though the tenant has possession, the landlord remains the owner. In most cases landlords do not object to such changes since the property will likely be improved.

Tenants are warned that they should undertake such improvements with caution since they may inadvertently be giving their landlord a gift by doing so. A **fixture** is an improvement on property that is fairly permanent in nature. Improvements that attach to the building and cannot be easily removed become fixtures. Decks, built-in bookcases, and toilets are all fixtures. The rule to be wary of is this: a tenant is not legally allowed to remove a fixture when she moves out. Thus, *fixtures become the property of the landlord.*

If, however, the improvement can be fairly easily removed, such as a chandelier or a satellite dish, then it is not a fixture and can be taken when the tenant moves. It is sometimes difficult to determine whether an improvement is an immovable fixture or a removable addition. If the improvement can be easily detached without harming the building, then it is not a fixture.

The Important Legal Concept to Remember: Once a tenant moves into a unit, the place is hers, and *everyone* needs her permission to enter. Because of the rule of fixtures, it is probably unwise for tenants to make major improvements to the property.

6

THE IMPLIED WARRANTY OF HABITABILITY (THE TENANT'S RIGHT TO A HABITABLE HOME)

Understanding the implied warranty of habitability
What the warranty means
Solutions for breach of the warranty of habitability

UNDERSTANDING THE IMPLIED WARRANTY OF HABITABILITY.
It is a tenant's worst nightmare. He moves into a seemingly
beautiful garden apartment and nothing works. The hot water
runs cold. The cold water does not run. The refrigerator leaks.
What is he to do? He should call the landlord and demand
that everything be fixed, pursuant to the implied warranty of
habitability.

The implied warranty of habitability is a clause implied in
every residential rental agreement. Basically, the warranty mandates that a landlord must make the unit fit for residential occupation, and that he maintain and repair all problems that make
the place unlivable.

The name says it all. First, the warranty is *implied*. It is part
of every rental agreement, whether or not it is specifically mentioned. It is part of month-to-month agreements as well as year-
long leases. It covers all residential rentals. In fact, it is highly

unlikely that your lease or rental agreement will even mention the warranty.

Yours may actually say the opposite. A clause that states something like "This lease expressly repeals the implied warranty of habitability" or something to the effect that the unit is being rented "as is" or that the landlord is relieved of any duty to maintain the premises is illegal and unenforceable. It is legal only in commercial (i.e., business) agreements, where there is no warranty of habitability. In all other cases, the warranty is implied in every rental contract, despite what the contract says. Because it is implied in every rental agreement, *this is probably the only time when you can absolutely ignore what the agreement states*. The warranty is implied in every contract, no matter what the contract says.

Next, notice that it is an implied *warranty*. A warranty is a statement or representation that something is true. In essence, a warranty is a promise. By renting the apartment to you, your landlord is making certain promises. What is he promising? That the unit is *habitable*—the third part of the equation.

"Habitable" means that the unit is fit to live in. It means that it is safe and sanitary. That it is structurally sound. That there is heat and hot water. That the toilet and plumbing work. It means that the windows are not cracked, and that the doors lock. Rats, rodents, cockroaches, and insect infestation are absent. It means that all building and health and safety codes are being met. This is not an exhaustive list by any means; any condition that makes the premises uninhabitable is covered. Habitable means that the unit is fit to live in.

Because every residential unit is covered by the implied warranty, any problem that affects the habitability of the home becomes the landlord's responsibility. This would include such items as a broken heater, refrigerator, or toilet, as well as something like a frayed electrical wire. Less severe things—normal wear and tear, as it were—may also be your landlord's responsibility to repair, depending upon the circumstances. (See Chapter 13, "The Duty to Maintain and Repair the Premises.")

After Marla had lived in her apartment for two years, the carpet had become a bit matted. She demanded that her landlord recarpet the place pursuant to the implied warranty of habitability. Her landlord refused, stating that carpet had nothing to do with habitability. Marla then withheld part of her rent in protest, and her landlord sued to evict her. The judge agreed that carpeting was not a habitability issue. Marla had to pay her landlord more than $2,000 in back rent, fees, and costs.

WHAT THE WARRANTY MEANS. The implied warranty of habitability means that the landlord must offer the dwelling to the new tenant in good shape. Before a tenant moves in, the unit must be fit for human habitation. It should be clean, sanitary, safe, and functioning. After a tenant moves in, the unit must be kept that way.

Sometimes, very rarely, a habitability problem will arise that is not the landlord's responsibility. This occurs only when the tenant, or someone the tenant knows, has created the habitability problem. Alternatively, if the problem was created by someone unknown to the tenant, then it is the landlord's job to fix it.

Denise was out shopping one day. When she came back to her apartment, she found the front window broken and her TV stolen.

Clearly, a broken window goes to the habitability of the apartment. Since it is fairly obvious that a stranger broke the window, it is Denise's landlord who is responsible for its repair.

About a month after the window was repaired, Denise's son was playing ball in front of the house. Not surprisingly, the ball went through the new window.

In this case, it is Denise's responsibility to repair the window, as it was her son who broke it. The landlord is liable for "third party" damage only if the third party is a stranger. The landlord is not responsible for problems that are caused by the tenant's **negligence**. If a tenant's child or friend causes the problem, it is up to the tenant to fix it. In all other cases, the duty to repair falls upon the shoulders of the landlord.

SOLUTIONS FOR BREACH OF THE WARRANTY OF HABITABILITY. The first thing a tenant must do is to figure out if the problem actually makes the dwelling *uninhabitable*. There are several factors that go into this determination:

1. When health, safety, or sanitation are in question;
2. When there has been a violation of a building, housing, or safety code;
3. When a vital part of the dwelling is affected;
4. When a consistent problem has not been fixed in a reasonable amount of time.

If a tenant suspects that the implied warranty of habitability is being violated, the next thing he must do is to notify the landlord of the problem and give him a reasonable amount of time to correct it. A landlord certainly cannot be held responsible for a problem he does not know about.

If the landlord refuses to fix the problem, the tenant should call the local authorities. Every city has some type of housing authority or health and public safety agency whose job it is to make sure that landlords are following the law. A call from them will certainly get your landlord's attention.

There are many other **remedies** that a tenant can also choose to use. The first is to withhold rent. This is called **rent abatement**. If a landlord is not living up to his end of the bargain, then the law allows the tenant to change the other end of the bargain. That is the theory behind rent abatement.

Here is how to utilize rent abatement: after you have deter-

mined that there has been a breach of the warranty of habitability, notify your landlord *in writing* of the problem and give him adequate time to fix the problem. If he does not fix it in a reasonable amount of time, notify him again *in writing* that you will be withholding rent the next month.

To withhold all of the rent or part of the rent—that is the question. The rule is that a tenant is allowed to withhold enough rent to make up for the problem. What is an apartment in New York worth in the winter without heat? Not much. The key is to pick a reasonable amount and stick to it.

After you withhold all or part of your landlord's rent, he will either fix the problem or **serve** you with an eviction notice. If he tries to evict you, it will ultimately be up to a judge to decide the proper amount of rent that should have been withheld. Sometimes keeping the entire rent until the problem is fixed is permissible, sometimes it is not. It all depends upon the severity and length of the problem. *Be sure to put whatever money you withhold in the bank.*

Maria's apartment lacked heat. She notified her landlord, Maggie, of the problem, but Maggie was too cheap to fix it. The next month, after proper notification, Maria withheld her entire $1,000 rent. Maria had put two months' rent in her savings account by the time Maggie's eviction lawsuit went before a judge. The judge ordered Maggie to fix the problem, but stated that Maria had no right to withhold her entire rent. He then ordered Maria to pay back Maggie $250 per month.

Had Maria spent that $2,000 instead of holding on to it, she likely would have had a difficult time paying Maggie the $500. If she failed to pay it, she would have been properly evicted.

The next option is often the best one. It is called **repair and deduct**. Repair and deduct operates on the same principle as rent withholding. The tenant keeps part of the rent in order to compensate for a **breach** by the landlord. However, instead of waiting to go to court and having a judge order the landlord to fix the problem, the tenant uses the withheld money to actually fix the problem himself (or he hires someone to fix it).

Mike had complained about his cold-running shower for a week, and still his landlord, Kevin, refused to fix it. Mike decided to solve the matter himself and called a plumber. The plumber came, fixed the problem, and charged Mike $85. Mike deducted the amount from his rent the next month.

Before a tenant decides to repair and deduct, it is incumbent upon him to notify the landlord of the problem and allow a reasonable amount of time for repair. Once the landlord fails to fix it, the tenant can remedy the problem without any authorization from the landlord. When rent time rolls around again, the tenant should send his landlord the deducted rent along with the receipt for the repair. The two together should equal one rent payment.

There are several limitations to this solution. First, a tenant cannot deduct more than the cost of the repair. That is why you must document everything you do with letters, receipts, and invoices. Also, again, repair and deduct cannot be used if the problem was created by the tenant. Some states also limit the use of this remedy to once or twice in a twelve-month period. In many states, the cost of repair cannot exceed one month's rent.

Sometimes the problem is so severe that the tenant does not want to fix it. She just wants out of the apartment, out of the lease, out of the whole deal altogether. In that case, the best remedy is to **vacate and sue**. Like any contract, if one party to a rental arrangement substantially breaches the agreement, the other party has the right to cancel the rest of the contract. Thus, once a landlord has been notified of a problem with the unit that impairs its livability and he fails to remedy the situation, the tenant has the right to move out, *even if* he has a long-term lease.

Another term for this right to cancel the contract and move is constructive eviction. Because the landlord has failed to fix a substantial problem, the law presumes that he is, in essence, evicting his tenant by his inaction. The tenant has been "constructively" evicted. The tenant can move out without repercussion.

A tenant may also, but does not have to, sue his landlord. Should he succeed, he would be entitled to a rebate for rent paid while living in an unfit unit, monetary compensation for substandard housing, and moving costs. (See Section V, "Lawsuits.")

The Important Legal Concept to Remember: Every residential tenant has an absolute right to a habitable home.

7

THE IMPLIED COVENANT OF QUIET ENJOYMENT (THE TENANT'S RIGHT TO PRIVACY)

Understanding the implied covenant of quiet enjoyment
How the covenant may be breached
Solutions for the breach of the covenant of quiet enjoyment

UNDERSTANDING THE IMPLIED COVENANT OF QUIET ENJOY-MENT. Once a tenant moves into his new rental unit, he has the right to be left alone in the "quiet enjoyment" of his home. This is called the implied covenant of quiet enjoyment. The covenant essentially states that a tenant has the right to use the premises without interference by either the landlord or other tenants.

Basically, this means that neither the landlord nor anyone under the control of the landlord can disturb the tenant's right to enjoy the unit quietly. Whereas the right to possession means that the tenant has a right to privacy in his home, this implied covenant states that he is entitled to live there peaceably. That is what quiet enjoyment means.

Sherri lived in a ten-unit apartment house, and her neighbor Spencer just loved to play Broadway musicals loudly at all hours of the day and night. Although Sherri complained to her landlord, Chris, he refused to discuss the matter with Spencer, and allowed the racket to continue. Accordingly, Chris has breached the implied covenant of quiet enjoyment.

Like the implied warranty of habitability, the implied covenant of quiet enjoyment too is found in every lease or rental agreement, whether or not it is specifically mentioned. That is why it is called an "implied" covenant.

This implied covenant goes further than the implied warranty of habitability. While the habitability promise applies only to residential tenants, the covenant of quiet enjoyment applies equally to both residential and business tenants. It is very important to realize, however, that unlike the implied warranty of habitability, the implied covenant of quiet enjoyment can be *waived* in the rental agreement. That is, while the implied warranty of habitability is *always present,* no matter what the lease states, the implied covenant of quiet enjoyment can be nullified if the rental agreement so states. Tenants should beware of this in the "fine print."

HOW THE COVENANT MAY BE BREACHED: There are many ways a landlord can breach the covenant of quiet enjoyment. The first is by refusing to control other tenants in the building. This implied promise of quiet enjoyment is intended to give hard-working people who pay rent the right to be left alone. A landlord who refuses to rein in an out-of-control tenant violates the covenant of quiet enjoyment since loud, boisterous, or obnoxious tenants are the responsibility of the landlord.

But the problem must be severe for the landlord to be held liable. A merely annoying neighbor does not constitute a breach, nor does the wrongdoing of a neighbor across the way who does not rent from the landlord. The landlord must have control over the premises *and* the tenant, *and* the problem must be substantial for the breach to be attributable to the landlord.

Here are some other examples of breaches by the landlord of the implied covenant of quiet enjoyment:

- Preventing the tenant from using an allotted parking space.
- Attempting to fix a problem in the unit, but failing to finish the job in a reasonable amount of time.
- Interfering with the tenant's business.
- Terminating the lease without just cause.
- Entering the unit repeatedly without authorization.
- Allowing tenants to harass other tenants.

Finally, the covenant can be breached in a manner similar to a breach of the warranty of habitability. If the landlord's action, or failure to act, is so substantial as to make the unit unfit to live in, then the covenant of quiet enjoyment as well as the warranty of habitability have been violated. A broken heater is a good example. Lack of heat clearly makes the unit uninhabitable, but it also certainly interferes with the tenant's quiet enjoyment of the apartment. While it may be a technical point of law, it is still good to know. The more ammunition a tenant has, the better.

SOLUTIONS FOR THE BREACH OF THE COVENANT OF QUIET ENJOYMENT. Several remedies that are available for a breach of the warranty of habitability are not applicable to a breach of the covenant of quiet enjoyment. First, repair and deduct is not a viable option since usually there is nothing to repair. Nor is calling the authorities relevant; loud landlords or noisy neighbors usually do not constitute a violation of a statute or housing code.

If you are a tenant whose privacy is being invaded, the first possible remedy is rent abatement; withhold a portion of your rent for a short period of time. This is especially effective if the interference is fairly minimal. Try withholding a small portion of your rent for a month or two. Your landlord will probably try to solve the problem.

If the interference is more severe, you can also try withholding a more substantial amount of rent. This, though, is a risky proposition; an eviction lawsuit will inevitably soon follow, and a judge may not be sympathetic to your cause. Whereas a tenant without heat who withholds rent is both a legally and emotionally sympathetic plaintiff, the same cannot be said for a tenant who "merely" has a loud neighbor. What seems to you to be a clear breach of the covenant of quiet enjoyment may be considered nothing more than a petty annoyance to a judge. If you gamble incorrectly, you will likely end up having to pay your landlord's legal and court costs.

That is why the final option is sometimes the best option: move out and sue your landlord. As with a tenant whose unit is uninhabitable, a tenant whose quiet enjoyment has been interfered with can allege constructive eviction, terminate the lease, and sue. If a judge agrees that the tenant has been constructively evicted, the tenant is owed the difference between what she paid for the unit and what it was actually worth with the problem, along with other incidentals.

Debbie was unable to use the second bedroom of her rented home for six months because her landlord "never got around" to moving his belongings out of it. An exasperated Debbie finally moved out and sued her landlord for a breach of the covenant of quiet enjoyment. The judge awarded Debbie $4,000.

Here is how that was calculated:

Rent per agreement:	$750
Value of the unit with the problem:	$500
Number of months with the problem:	6
SUBTOTAL	$1,500
($250 a month x 6 months)	
Moving costs	$1,000
Deposit	$1,500
GRAND TOTAL DUE DEBBIE:	$4,000

Since the amount that a tenant can likely recover is fairly small, you are advised to file your claim in **small claims court**. Small claims cases are expeditious (a month or two from filing the suit to trial) and relatively inexpensive. (See Chapter 21, "Small Claims Court.")

The Important Legal Concept to Remember: Tenants have a right to be left alone.

8

THE DUTY TO PAY RENT

Payment of rent

Late rent payments

When payment of rent is excused

When can a landlord raise your rent?

Illegal rent increases due to retaliation or discrimination

Rent control

Many tenants resent paying their rent every month. Aside from the financial burden, they believe that their hard-earned cash is nothing but pure profit for their greedy, rich landlord. Unfortunately for the landlord, that is rarely the case.

While knowing where your money goes will not ease the financial pain that paying rent often inflicts, it may ease the emotional resentment. Your landlord likely spends your monthly rent as follows: 20 percent is paid in taxes, 65 percent is paid to the bank for the mortgage on the property, and 12 percent is spent on costs and upkeep on the rental unit. Probably only 3 percent of your monthly rent is considered profit. If your rent is $500 a month, that means that only $15 is your landlord's actual profit. So, have some compassion, if at all possible. When you are late with your rent, the bank may be breathing down your landlord's back and he may be cranky for a reason (although he may just be cranky altogether).

PAYMENT OF RENT. *Paying rent is the first and foremost duty of any tenant.* Excuses do not pay the mortgage, nor do bounced checks. Irresponsible roommates are not a reason not to pay rent, and neither is the need to buy a new mountain bike. The only reason a tenant even lives in the house or apartment, which is owned by the landlord, is because he promised to pay rent. Failure to pay rent in full consistently and on time will get you evicted. Paying rent is the first and foremost duty of any tenant.

Rent is normally paid monthly and is due on the first of every month, although a landlord and tenant can actually agree to any arrangement that they want. If you get paid on the fifth of every month, there is nothing preventing you and your landlord from agreeing to your rent being paid on the sixth. Some landlords want rent paid every two weeks. This too is legal.

If the day for paying rent falls on a weekend or a holiday, then it is typically legally permissible to pay it on the next business day. Note that while many landlords offer a three- to five-day "grace period" for paying rent, they are not required by law to do so.

Similarly, if you bounce a check to your landlord, he is not required to charge you a bounced-check fee and continue the relationship. Some landlords simply begin eviction proceedings (since a bounced check means that rent has not been paid), especially if there is a pattern of bounced checks. A tenant must pay rent—it is as simple as that.

Here's a good tip if you know you are going to have a difficult time paying rent one month: tell your landlord about your situation, and offer to make a partial rent payment. That is far better than possibly bouncing a check and hoping for the best. It is always far better to treat your landlord with respect, communicate well, and try to get along with him than to be a pain in the neck. You will find that your landlord will be far more willing to work with you when needed if you are a good tenant and normally pay your rent on time. If your landlord does agree to accept a partial rent payment one month, get the agreement in writing.

LATE RENT PAYMENTS. Landlords are well within their rights to charge a fee for a late rent payment. Fees for late rent are perfectly legal, although excessive fees may not be. What is "excessive"? That is a good question without a definitive answer. There are few laws that actually regulate the amount a landlord can charge for late rent. While $50 may be legal, $150 may not be.

If you think that your landlord charges too much in late fees, here's a trick that might work: any contract (not just a landlord-tenant agreement) that includes *grossly excessive* fees may be deemed **unconscionable** by a court. Unconscionable contracts, or sections of contracts, are unenforceable. You can always take your landlord to small claims court and get a judge to rule that the fee is excessive. But while such a decision could save you some money, it would also likely alienate your landlord. As with the rest of your relationship with your landlord, be aggressive, know your rights, but don't be stupid. Pick your battles wisely.

WHEN PAYMENT OF RENT IS EXCUSED. As indicated, paying rent is the most important duty a tenant has. There are, however, two times when failure to pay rent may be legally excused.

As explained in more detail in Chapter 6, "The Implied Warranty of Habitability," rent may be temporarily excused when a tenant elects to utilize the remedy called repair and deduct (you pay someone else to fix a problem and deduct that amount from your next month's rent).

The other time rent payments are possibly excused is when there is a substantial flaw in the unit and the tenant utilizes the remedy of rent abatement, withholding all or part of the rent. A judge will later determine whether the tenant had the right to withhold the rent. Other than repair and deduct or rent abatement, there is no other situation in which failure to pay rent is legally justifiable.

WHEN CAN A LANDLORD RAISE YOUR RENT? Whether your landlord can increase your rent depends upon the nature of your agreement. If you have a lease, your landlord cannot raise your rent, not even a penny, during the course of the agreement. From a tenant's point of view, that is one of the advantages of having a lease. If at the end of the lease you want to stay and your landlord wants you to also, then she can legally raise your rent at the beginning of the new term.

If you have a month-to-month agreement or some other sort of periodic tenancy, then your landlord *can* raise your rent, but only after giving the proper notice. The amount of notice required corresponds to the payment of rent. If rent is due every thirty days, then thirty days' notice is required to raise your rent. If it is due every two weeks, then two weeks' notice is all that is needed to raise rent.

There is no set limit as to how much a landlord can charge for rent. She can charge whatever the market will bear. If she raises rents too high, her tenants will move out and she will have a problem re-letting the space. The only time a rent increase is prohibited is when rent control (also known as rent stabilization) is in effect or if the increase is either retaliatory or discriminatory.

ILLEGAL RENT INCREASES DUE TO RETALIATION OR DISCRIMI-NATION. It is illegal for a landlord to raise a tenant's rent simply because the tenant has exercised some legal right.

Rebecca could no longer wait for her landlord to fix the oven in the house she rented. She finally hired a handyman and had the appliance repaired. She deducted the amount of repair from her next month's rent. Rebecca received a termination notice the following day.

Rebecca's landlord's actions are patently illegal. Raising rent because a tenant organized a tenants' union, for example, is illegal, as would be any increase directly related to a tenant utilizing a legal landlord-tenant remedy.

In a similar vein, a landlord cannot raise a tenant's rent

because of that tenant's race, ethnicity, religion, sex, etc. It violates federal and state civil rights laws, and is just another form of illegal discrimination. Any rent increase based upon a discriminatory purpose is illegal.

Proving retaliation or discrimination is not always easy, but a tenant who feels that she has had her rent increased for improper reasons should not let the increase go by without some sort of retaliation of her own. A variety of remedies are available:

- *Complain to the proper authorities:* Often, complaining to the proper local, state, or federal housing authorities will put enough fear into a landlord to reverse the illegal rent increase. When you do complain, make sure to send a copy of your letter to your landlord.
- *Organize a rent strike:* A **rent strike** is an organized effort on the part of tenants designed to put financial pressure on the landlord by withholding everyone's rent. Few landlords can afford to go without their rent for more than a month. (See Chapter 11, "Other Tenant Solutions.")
- *Sue:* If you are being treated unfairly and illegally, you can always sue in either state or federal court. A federal antidiscriminatory suit is called a civil rights suit. It is expensive both to pursue and to defend. (See Chapter 22, "Superior Court.")

A final option is simply to refuse to pay the increase. When that happens, your landlord will try to evict you. It is important to know that legally it is your landlord's responsibility (called his **burden of proof**) to prove that the increase was not discriminatory or retaliatory. In fact, in many cases, the law presumes that an arbitrary rent increase was improper. Your landlord will have to present sufficient evidence that the increase was reasonable, and not spiteful.

RENT CONTROL. The basic intent of rent control (laws that restrict the amount of rent a landlord can charge) is to slow rent increases. Rent control does not mean that a landlord cannot raise rent at all. What it does mean is that the amount he can raise it is regulated by statute. In some cities, landlords are permitted to raise rents yearly, but the amount that rent can be raised is limited. Typically, rents in these places can be raised between 4 and 9 percent each year. In other cities, landlords are required to go before a local rent-control board to get permission before rent can be raised. In cities with ordinances like these, rental increases are usually tied to inflation and interest rates. Tenants who are covered by rent control need to get a copy of their local ordinance and acquaint themselves with the law so that they can know what type of rent increases are legally permissible in their area.

If you believe that your rent has been increased more than is legally permissible in your city, you need to take your complaint before your local rent-control board. A rent-control board hearing is not all that much different from a hearing before a judge, albeit you will be presenting your "case" before a panel of people rather than a single jurist. The key to both is to be well prepared and to be able to prove your case with **evidence**—witnesses, letters, documents, receipts, etc. Make sure to read Chapter 21, "Small Claims Court," to get a better idea about how to approach such a hearing.

The Important Legal Concept to Remember: Renters must pay rent; nonpayment is rarely excused.

9

THE TENANT'S DUTY TO BEHAVE REASONABLY

The duty to keep the unit in good condition

The tenant cannot commit waste

The tenant cannot be a nuisance

The tenant cannot use the rental for unintended purposes

There are, unfortunately, too many tenants who push the limits of acceptable behavior. Tenants who know that they can stop paying rent and still stay in the unit until a judge tells them they have to leave. But there are consequences to such actions. Many jurisdictions allow a landlord to collect money damages, as well as attorney fees and costs, from the tenant who violates the standards set forth below.

THE DUTY TO KEEP THE UNIT IN GOOD CONDITION. The law imposes upon landlords the responsibility to maintain and repair normal wear and tear in the unit, and this makes sense. If a dryer breaks after ten years of normal use, it should not be the unfortunate tenant who needed to dry her laundry one day who should pay for it. Landlords repair normal wear and tear.

But they do not have to fix problems not of their making. Any extraordinary damage to the unit is the tenant's duty to fix.

Larry and his college roommate Tim were wrestling in the den one day. Larry threw Tim against the wall, the wall broke, and Tim fell through. It is Larry and Tim's responsibility to fix the wall.

It would also be Larry and Tim's responsibility to repair the wall if it were broken by someone they knew. Problems caused by tenants and their guests are the tenants' responsibility.

THE TENANT CANNOT COMMIT WASTE. A tenant not only has a duty to repair whatever significant problems he creates, but has a further duty not to allow the unit to fall into disrepair. This is known as the doctrine of **waste**. Although a tenant has exclusive control of the unit, it is still the landlord's property. Accordingly, a duty is imposed upon the tenant by law that says that he cannot decrease the value of the property.

Tom loved to fix old cars. As time went by, he collected several on the front lawn of the home he leased, none of which worked. Neighbors started complaining. His landlord demanded that the cars be removed. Tom was committing waste.

Waste means that a tenant has an obligation not to let the property fall apart. While this may seem to contradict the rule that a landlord has a duty to repair the premises, they really are two different things. The duty to repair means that the landlord must keep the unit habitable. The duty not to commit waste means that the tenant has an obligation not to harm the property. While a landlord might welcome a new coat of paint on the house he is renting out, he might not if the tenant paints it purple. That is waste.

THE TENANT CANNOT BE A NUISANCE. As indicated earlier, all tenants have a right to the quiet enjoyment of their rental property. Not only does this mean that they have a right to privacy but it also means that they have a right to live in relative peace and quiet. A tenant who disturbs another's quiet enjoyment is a **nuisance**, and a landlord has a right to rid his property of any nuisances. The tenant who stays awake at all hours blasting his stereo will be facing an eviction in a short amount of time.

Many different types of actions can constitute an illegal nuisance. A tenant cannot, for example, allow his trash area to become unsanitary. A tenant cannot allow her garden to grow so out of control that her neighbor cannot use his driveway. Any action or inaction that significantly impairs another tenant's use and enjoyment of her dwelling would be considered a nuisance.

THE TENANT CANNOT USE THE RENTAL FOR UNINTENDED PURPOSES. A landlord has a right to have his property used for its intended purpose. For example:

- A tenant cannot allow six more family members to move into her two-bedroom house after she has moved in. A landlord has every right to expect that a two-bedroom home will house no more than four or five people.

- A tenant cannot normally run a business out of a residential property unless she has the express prior written approval of the landlord. The intended purpose of a residence is to reside.

- A tenant cannot participate in any illegal activity in the space. Selling drugs and prostitution are definite no-no's.

A tenant who violates any of these duties will give her landlord just cause for eviction.

The Important Legal Concept to Remember: With rights come responsibilities. If a tenant is irresponsible and behaves in an unreasonable manner, the law will protect the landlord's right to get rid of the tenant.

10

SECURITY DEPOSITS AND LAST MONTH'S RENT

Security deposits in general

The important differences between deposits, fees, and last month's rent

How to make sure your security deposit is returned

If the deposit is not returned

SECURITY DEPOSITS IN GENERAL. A security deposit is money paid by the tenant and held by the landlord to make sure that the tenant performs all obligations under the lease or rental agreement. In that sense, security deposits are like a form of insurance. If a tenant fails to live up to certain obligations under the agreement, the deposit (or a portion thereof) is forfeited to the landlord to pay for these things. Generally, security deposits can be used only to clean the unit, to repair damage to the unit above and beyond normal wear and tear, or to pay for unpaid back rent.

It is important for both tenants and landlords to understand that a security deposit is the *property of the tenant*. Yes, it is held by the landlord. Yes, the landlord has the right to keep part of it if the tenant acts improperly. But until the end of the tenancy, and until the landlord can justify keeping all or part of it, the deposit is the tenant's money.

By definition, then, a security deposit is refundable. As long as the tenant pays rent, keeps the premises in good condition, and leaves the place clean, the deposit should be fully refunded. Any agreement that states that the deposit is nonrefundable is illegal and unenforceable against the tenant. *A security deposit belongs to the tenant and is refundable.*

Different localities set different amounts that can be charged as a security deposit. Usually, the amount of the deposit will equal between one and three months' rent. Deposits for more than that amount are probably illegal, although, again, it depends upon where you live.

For many tenants, paying the security deposit on top of rent often makes moving into a new rental unit difficult. Here's a method that allows tenants to pay a large security deposit more easily while also permitting landlords to collect the maximum deposit allowed by law: allow the tenant to pay the deposit over a period of several months.

Eve wanted to rent a house from Francesco. The problem was not that Francesco wanted $500 a month for the place; instead, it was that he wanted a $1,500 security deposit, which was permissible in the city they lived in. Rather than lose a potential good tenant like Eve, Francesco offered Eve the option to pay the deposit over a six-month period. For her first six months in the house, Eve paid her regular $500 monthly rent payment, along with an extra $250 a month toward her security deposit.

This plan gives the tenant some breathing room and allows the landlord to collect the maximum possible deposit allowed by law.

THE IMPORTANT DIFFERENCES BETWEEN FEES, DEPOSITS, AND LAST MONTH'S RENT. You should know the difference between fees, security deposits, and last month's rent, as they are three distinctly different animals.

Fees are payments for a service, and requiring a fee for a service rendered is normally legal. A credit-check fee, for example, is usually permissible. As opposed to a deposit, a fee belongs to the landlord and is nonrefundable, although it is illegal to charge a fee for something that is already covered by a security deposit. A common abuse occurs when a landlord requires a security deposit and also asks for a "cleaning fee." Since security deposits cover cleaning costs, charging an extra fee for cleaning is prohibited in most jurisdictions.

Last month's rent is different too. While a security deposit can be used for a variety of things when a tenant moves out, last month's rent can be used only to pay the last month's rent. That is it. A landlord who is holding a $500 security deposit and $500 in last month's rent actually has only $500 to rectify any problems the tenant may cause. Legally, that other $500 can only be applied to a last rent payment.

Laws in most cities restrict the total amount of money a landlord can hold, whether it is called last month's rent or security deposit. So, even though a prepaid last month's rent is not a refundable deposit, if a landlord collects last month's rent he limits the total amount of security deposit he can also collect. For landlords, the problem with that is if something major goes wrong, a landlord cannot legally use the last month's rent money to fix the porblem. So, here is a critical tip for landlords: *The smart landlord should always call all retained money a security deposit so that the money can be used for any legal purpose.*

Jay rented an apartment from David. When Jay moved in, David required $500 in first month's rent, $500 in last month's rent, and a $250 security deposit. Jay lived there for six months and then gave proper notice of his intent to move. He did not pay his last month's rent pursuant to the agreement, and then moved out. After Jay left, David learned that Jay's cat had ruined the carpet and it needed to be completely replaced. The $250 deposit hardly covered David's costs.

Had David asked for a $750 security deposit instead of $500 in last month's rent and a $250 security deposit, Jay would have paid rent that last month, and David would have had enough money to pay for the new carpet.

It is also good practice for a landlord to get as much money up front as is legally permissible. Not only will this give him enough money to fix almost any problem that may arise, but it will also induce the tenant to be as good as possible since she will want to get her money back. Tenants with small deposits have little to lose by breaking the rules.

HOW TO MAKE SURE YOUR SECURITY DEPOSIT IS RETURNED. Again, the security deposit is owned by the tenant, even if it is rarely treated that way. A landlord cannot keep it without justification. Tenants, then, should give their landlord no reason to keep their money.

Any tenant who wants his security deposit returned is advised to abide by the following five rules:

Rule 1. *Give proper notice of your intent to move:* Your landlord can keep deposit money for lost rent if you move without giving proper notice. If you have a month-to-month rental arrangement and you give less than thirty days' notice, you should fully expect your landlord to keep part of the deposit. So, don't do it.

Rule 2. *Pay all rent due:* If you do not pay your last month's rent, your landlord can legally keep as much of your security deposit as necessary to make up for it.

Rule 3. *Fix what you broke:* Since your landlord can legally retain part of your deposit to repair damage to the unit that is not considered normal wear and tear, be sure to make all needed repairs.

Rule 4. *Leave the unit spotless:* Your landlord can subtract deposit money to clean the premises. If you make sure to clean it thoroughly before you leave, this will not be necessary.

Rule 5. *Document what you have done:* After you have fixed and cleaned everything, be sure to document that you have left the unit in good condition. Photograph or videotape the unit after you have moved everything out. It is also a good idea to have a walk-through with your landlord on the day you leave. To be really safe, bring a friend along; if you later have to sue your landlord to get your deposit back, your friend will be an invaluable witness.

Aside from rent, cleaning, and repairs, your landlord cannot use your deposit for any other reason. In most localities, landlords are obliged to return the deposit to the tenant within a fairly short period of time, usually four weeks. At that time, if any of the deposit is withheld, as it usually is, landlords are obliged to give their tenants an itemized statement of how the money was used. By following the five rules above, you stand a far greater chance that your entire deposit will be returned.

IF THE DEPOSIT IS NOT RETURNED. Many places require a landlord to return the security deposit with interest, but it is the lucky tenant indeed who ever sees a security deposit returned with interest. It is not unusual for a landlord to keep all or part of a security deposit without reason.

If your landlord has not returned what you believe to be enough of your money, you have two options. You can either sue him in small claims court (or "housing court," if one exists in your area), or you can try to threaten him with a demand letter, which, surprisingly, works if done correctly.

Attorneys write demand letters all the time. The reason lawyers find these letters successful is because recipients decide that the financial consequences of not doing as demanded are not worth the risk. A person who receives a letter from a lawyer demanding $100 often decides that it is simply cheaper to pay the money than to hire an attorney and fight back. The lawyer's letter induces fear. Yours can too.

Your letter to your landlord must explain in simple terms why you are entitled to a return of your money. Set forth the facts of what happened simply and without emotion. Then let your landlord know that you know the law. Explain why you are legally entitled to a return of your deposit—the unit was left clean, you paid your rent, nothing was broken, etc.

If your letter is to be at all effective, you must also create some fear in your landlord. Tell your landlord that you have *proof* that the unit was left in proper condition. Tell him that you have photos and witnesses. Tell him that if he does not return your deposit within three business days, you will sue in small claims court. Tell him that not only will he then have to return your money with interest but he may get hit with a fine as well.

It is this threat of a credible lawsuit that may return your money. You have to be correct—you have to have left the place clean, paid all rent, etc. If there is a legitimate dispute, your landlord will probably decide to take his chances and let a judge resolve the matter. But if you are right, and if you can show your greedy landlord that you can prove you are right, he may just decide to return your money. Without a credible threat based upon facts in your favor, do not expect to see your money returned by using this method.

If the letter does not work, sue him. Chapter 21, "Small Claims Court," explains how to prepare and present a case in small claims or housing court. That is what you will need to do if you are to get your money back.

The Important Legal Concept to Remember: A security deposit is the property of the tenant and must be returned unless there are good reasons to keep it.

11

OTHER TENANT SOLUTIONS

Negotiations and mediation

Lawsuits

Tenants' unions or associations

How to organize

Your final options

When it gets to the point where a tenant feels she must take some action against her landlord in order to rectify a problem, there are a variety of legal tools available. Happily, many of these solutions do not require the assistance of an attorney. Please note that if the problem you face has to do with a breach of either the warranty of habitability or the covenant of quiet enjoyment, solutions to those particular issues are dealt with in Chapter 6 and Chapter 7, respectively.

NEGOTIATIONS AND MEDIATION. The very easiest, least adversarial, most inexpensive solution to many landlord-tenant problems is simply to try to work things out with your landlord. In fact, it is often in his best interest to work things out with you. Landlords know that tenants now have a variety of legal solutions they can employ. They also know that a disgruntled tenant or a vacant apartment means no rent. There are few things landlords like less than no rent. Accordingly, you may find that your landlord may be far more willing to replace that refrigerator than you think.

Negotiations with a landlord need not be intimidating. The key to a successful negotiation is twofold. First, be reasonable. Try to be nice and accommodating. Listen to your landlord and try to give him something. If he wants rent paid on time, then promise to really try to pay your rent on time. Acting reasonably costs you nothing and generates goodwill.

But goodwill all by itself rarely works. It is when you add a credible threat to your reasonableness that good solutions appear. Make sure your landlord understands that you know your rights, and that you will utilize your rights if necessary. This means that he knows that you may withhold rent and possibly sue if things cannot be worked out. Conveying a viable threat that will hit him in the wallet will give your landlord a great incentive to settle with you. A new refrigerator is far less expensive than three months' lost rent.

Sometimes a more formal approach is needed. If your chat with your landlord failed to produce your desired results, another option is mediation.

Liz was three months into a year-long lease when a dispute about her rose garden erupted with her landlord, Dan. They fought for months. Liz really liked the house and wanted to renew the lease when it ran out, yet she knew that Dan would never do that until the "rose war" ended. She swallowed her pride, called Dan one day, and asked, "Do you want to go to mediation to see if we can resolve this problem?" Dan was happy to agree.

Mediation is a nonadversarial process that attempts to bridge gaps, find common ground, and resolve differences. Mediators are neutral individuals whose job it is to assist the parties in creating an agreement that works for everybody. And, while permissible, attorneys need not be present.

Mediation works. It is a flexible process that can be used to settle major wars or minor skirmishes. Mediation is also a confidential process. Whatever is said to the mediator will be kept private, and whatever results are reached (good or bad) will also remain confidential. It should also be fairly inexpensive. Many communities have free, or at least very inexpensive, mediation and dispute-resolution centers. Look in the phone book under those topics or call a local law school.

After finding a mediator, a mutually acceptable time for the mediation will be set. The mediation may take an hour or a day—once the issues involved are made clear to the mediator, he or she can estimate how long it will take.

Most mediations will proceed something like this: at the scheduled time and date the mediator will likely bring both parties and their attorneys, if they have any, into one room for an opening session. This beginning session allows each party to state his or her point of view about the situation and provides the mediator with necessary background information.

The mediator will probably next put each party in a separate room and continue the process by conducting a type of "shuttle diplomacy," whereby he goes back and forth between the rooms, prodding, cajoling, pulling, and sometimes yanking the parties toward a resolution based upon compromise. If successful, the parties will agree to resolve their differences and end their dispute.

LAWSUITS. If meditation and negotiations have failed, then things are pretty dire in your neck of the woods. At this point, you essentially have three choices left. First, you could give up and move. Second, you could form a tenants' association (discussed below). Finally, you could opt to use the most commonly thought of solution to most legal problems: filing suit.

There are two types of lawsuits that a tenant can file against a landlord. If the problem is relatively minor and the amount in dispute is less than, say, $5,000 (the amount depends upon which state you live in), then you should file suit in small claims court.

If the dispute is more serious and the amount in controversy exceeds $5,000, then you need to file suit in a **superior court** (also known as municipal court, county court, or district court). Small claims actions can be done without the aid of an attorney, while a superior court lawsuit necessitates legal counsel. Both are discussed in detail in Section V, "Lawsuits."

TENANTS' UNIONS OR ASSOCIATIONS. When all else fails—when after negotiations, mediation, and rent abatement a significant problem still exists—it is time to consider forming a tenants' union, and then using, if necessary, probably the most potent tool in the tenant arsenal: a rent strike.

A tenants' association or union is not unlike a labor union. It is a group of people acting together to effectuate change. The concept is the same, only the actors change. Labor unions are in existence because individual laborers sometimes have a more difficult time negotiating with management than does a group of employees acting together. Similarly, tenants may find their landlord more responsive when twenty of them show up together with the same grievance.

There is great power in uniting, acting, and negotiating as a single unit. It is much more difficult for a landlord to lie, break promises, and bamboozle his tenants when they are sharing information and acting together. If your building lacks substantial necessities, such as proper lighting, heat, smoke alarms, or hot water; if your landlord takes too long to fix a problem (if he fixes it at all); if the complex is unsanitary; or if you simply feel that the building needs to be run more professionally, then forming a tenants' union makes sense.

The central heat and air-conditioning unit for the Meadowview apartments broke one November day. It was not the first time this had happened. The management did nothing to fix it for several days. Bob was fed up and knew that withholding his rent alone would provide little incentive for the management to fix the heater. Instead, he printed up some flyers and organized a tenants' meeting. About half of the tenants showed up. He suggested that they *all* threaten to withhold rent if the heater was not fixed in a day, and he convinced the angry yet skeptical crowd to go along with his plan. Everyone there signed a petition to that effect that night. The heater was fixed the next day.

Rents are the lifeblood of a landlord's business. While an individual rent withholding or repair and deduct might be annoying, it certainly does not threaten the landlord's business. But in the case of the Meadowview, if an average rent payment is $500 and fifty tenants threaten to withhold rent, the owner stands to lose $25,000 *that month alone*. A landlord could go out of business and lose his building very quickly if a rent strike went unchecked. Rent strikes level the playing field.

HOW TO ORGANIZE. Organizing is a labor-intensive endeavor. It will require a lot of work at first, and a lot of work later on. But it should be worth it.

Organizing usually begins when there is a problem that everyone is aware of but no one is doing anything about. If you are interested in starting a tenants' association, here is one way to do it: begin by talking with a few people you know well and see if they want to help organize a general meeting to discuss the problem. Go door-to-door and try to get at least ten to fifteen people to come to the meeting. Hold the meeting in your apartment.

This first meeting is informal. It is a chance to share ideas, explain the benefits of organizing, and get to know one another. As the host, you should speak first. Explain who you are, your history at the building, and your perception of the problem(s). Everyone there should do the same. Compare notes, share experiences, and come up with a tentative game plan. If everyone agrees to continue, then plan the second meeting.

Between the first and second meeting two things need to

occur. First, the rest of the complex needs to be made aware of what happened at the first get-together and should be encouraged to show up at the second meeting. It is critical to get as many people involved as possible. You cannot have too many members, but you sure can have too few; the strength of organizing is in the numbers. In a small building, you need virtually every tenant to join the union for it to be effective.

If at all possible, you should also try to find a representative from another tenants' union in your area to come speak at the second gathering. Tenants' unions are hard to find—they do not advertise or make much noise outside the complex. Go to a few well-established, large apartment complexes in your area and see if you can locate a union. Call some local tenant attorneys. Contact a local labor union. Legal-aid offices and media outlets may also be good sources for locating tenants' unions in your city.

The second meeting is used to set priorities, elect officers (president, vice president, secretary), and spread the gospel. What is the purpose of the union? Stopping frequent rent increases? Improving sanitation? Getting a specific problem fixed? It is imperative to try to get some sort of consensus. If you have a representative from another union there, have her explain how her union began. Depending upon the circumstances and size of the union, collecting dues may even be warranted. Dues are used to hire competent legal counsel.

Besides officers, section leaders should be elected for each floor or section of the building. These officers help to keep everyone informed and energized. The keys to a tenants' union are strength in numbers and *solidarity*. You must act together and stay unified. That is where section leaders come in. They are your troops.

Make sure that no members of the building management or their employees come to this meeting, or to any of your meetings, for that matter. This is your union—management need not apply. Management should, however, be informed of the existence of the union and its officers. At the conclusion of the second or third meeting, your landlord should be advised to expect a list of issues to be discussed.

After the union has been organized, the next meeting or two should be used to come up with a formal list of demands. You cannot begin to discuss issues with your landlord until you know exactly what you want, and how far your group is willing to go.

It is a very tense situation when you get to a place where a rent strike is looming. Is everyone prepared for that? Are they willing to live with the stress? As mentioned several times previously, it is the credible threat that often induces change. Unless your group is willing to go all the way, your threat of a rent strike, which should induce fear, may instead seem hollow.

The officers, or a standing committee, should be empowered to negotiate with management on all the tenants' behalf. It is then time to go meet with your landlord.

Have the officers or negotiations committee take the list of demands to your landlord to see if a compromise can be reached. Be friendly, but not too friendly. Be serious, but not bombastic. Make sure your landlord understands that if your demands are not met, a rent strike will be forthcoming. It is the credible threat that will force him to take you seriously.

At the same time, be sure to contact the appropriate government agency. Health departments and building departments have staff ready to investigate your complaint. It is also a very good idea to send a press release to local television, radio, and newspaper news departments.

YOUR FINAL OPTIONS. If negotiations fail to solve the problem, then the final two options are either to collectively repair and deduct or to collectively withhold rent. In a repair and deduct situation, part of each member's rent money is paid to the union instead of the landlord, and the union spends the money to fix the problem. The advantage of a community repair and deduct is that when large amounts of money are collected, large items can be fixed.

It is critical to keep immaculate records. Members of the union as well as the judge who may eventually review what has happened will want to see what the union did with the money it received.

When one person withholds his rent, it is called rent abatement. When an entire building withholds rent, it is called a rent strike. It is the tenants' ultimate weapon. A rent strike is a very serious matter and should not be attempted by the faint of heart. It should be used only as a last resort, when all else fails. By the time the union is contemplating a rent strike, it needs to have hired a good tenants' attorney to help it through the crisis.

Participating members should pay their entire rent to the union instead of their landlord, and the union should then deposit the money in its bank account. As all or part of that money will eventually need to be paid to the landlord, it is critical that your members do not just go and spend their rent one month instead of paying it to the union.

The ultimate goal, whether it is reached by negotiations or by a rent strike, is a written agreement between the landlord and the union. This is sometimes called a collective bargaining agreement. The agreement will recognize the union as the legitimate bargaining entity for the tenants. It will also spell out what the landlord has agreed to do and when he will do it.

Finally, recall that retaliatory evictions are illegal. A landlord cannot evict any tenant merely because the tenant joins or participates in the union or its activities.

The Important Legal Concept to Remember: While it is usually better for everyone concerned if problems can be resolved amicably, that is not always possible. It is the credible threat that most often induces change.

LANDLORD RIGHTS, DUTIES, AND SOLUTIONS

12

LANDLORD RIGHTS

Ensuring that rent is paid
The right to have reasonable tenants
The right of entry
The right to change rental agreement terms

It is important to understand that when rights are mentioned, be they landlord rights or tenant rights, duties soon follow. Rights and responsibilities are flip sides of the landlord-tenant coin. When, for example, it is said that a landlord has a right to have reasonable tenants, it follows that tenants have a corresponding duty to behave reasonably. When a tenant has a right to a habitable home, the landlord has a responsibility to make sure it is habitable. That is the very nature of landlord-tenant law. Rights and duties go hand in hand.

ENSURING THAT RENT IS PAID. The first right a landlord has corresponds with a tenant's foremost duty—the duty to pay, and the right to receive, rent. Renting property is a business, and the purpose of business is to make money. The money a landlord makes comes from rent. No tenant would expect to be able to walk into a store and leave with a new pair of pants with only a promise to pay "real soon." That simply does not happen. Landlords have every right to expect that rent will be paid in full and on time. If it is not, the tenant will not be living in the unit for long.

It is good practice for a landlord to have a firm policy to ensure that rent is paid promptly. Rent should be due on the first of the month. It should be considered late no later than the fifth. Failure to pay by the fifth should result in a **Notice to Pay Rent or Quit**. (See Chapter 16, "Landlord Solutions.") While there is nothing wrong with working things out with a tenant you like, it is usually far better to have a firm policy to deviate from when need be instead of having deviation be the norm.

Here are three other ways to make sure rent is paid promptly:

1. *Late fees:* This is a simple and well-known policy that tenants do not like. The landlord sets the date for rent payments, sets the date when rent will be considered late, and sets the amount the tenant will pay if rent is late. If you decide to use this method, make sure it is made part of your rental agreement so that no one is surprised when the late fee is assessed.

2. *Discounts for timely payments:* This is a more user-friendly approach. Here, the tenant gets a discount of, say, $20 if the rent is paid on time. The key is to *add $20 extra into the price you would normally charge for rent* initially so that you are not really giving a discount at all, although your happy tenant will feel like you are.

3. *Evictions:* If word gets around the complex that you evict rent scofflaws, you soon won't have many.

A landlord also has a right to raise rent as he or she sees fit. Again, as long as there are no rent control laws prohibiting rent increases, as long as tenants are willing to pay the higher rent, as long as no lease is involved, and as long as proper notice has been given, there is nothing improper about a rent increase. Raising rent should not be taken lightly, though. Many landlords dislike rent increases; tenants get mad and vacancies occur. If a rent increase is necessary, be sure to do the following:

- *Give ample warning:* Let your tenants know informally that rent will have to be raised and when the increase will likely take effect. Here's a way to make this act more palatable: when you tell your tenants about the possible raise, inflate the amount by 10 percent. When you do raise the rents, and do so at a price that is 10 percent less than your tenants feared, it will not seem as bad.

- *Give proper notification:* All rent increases should be in writing, and should state the name of the tenant and the number of the unit, the amount of the old and new rent, and the date when the increase will be effective. Try to hand-deliver the notification if at all possible. As improper notification is cause to disregard the increase, at least for a month, be sure to give more than enough lead time. Six weeks is a good idea.

THE RIGHT TO HAVE REASONABLE TENANTS. Landlords have a right to expect that tenants will behave in a reasonable fashion. Even though a tenant has exclusive possession of the unit throughout the tenancy, he cannot treat the unit in a way that will harm it or decrease its value. In legal terms, that means that the tenant cannot commit waste. He cannot harm the structure, paint it purple—that sort of thing.

Acting reasonably also means that the tenant cannot use the apartment for anything other than its expected use.

J.J. signed a residential lease with Leonard. After he moved in, J.J. started to run his photography business out of the duplex. People were constantly coming and going from the house, picking up pictures and sitting for photo sessions. After warning J.J. several times, and even though the lease had eight months to run, Leonard served J.J. with an eviction notice, and the eviction was upheld in court.

The right to reasonable tenants also means that landlords have a right to have tenants who do not disturb the quiet enjoyment of other tenants. Constant loud parties, daily band practice, and nightly shouting matches are all examples of inappropriate tenant behavior that violate this right.

Finally, it is patently illegal for a tenant to participate in illegal activities in the rental. Selling drugs, engaging in prostitution, and the like, are activities that are legally outside the bounds of reasonable behavior and are justifiable grounds for eviction.

THE RIGHT OF ENTRY. Although a house is a tenant's castle while she lives there, even a castle sometimes needs attention. The right to exclusive possession and quiet enjoyment of a home is thus not an unconditional right. As the owner, the landlord retains the right to enter the premises when necessary, albeit in a limited capacity. Generally speaking, there are three times when a landlord can enter the premises:

1. *With permission:* A landlord can always enter the unit when given permission to do so by the tenant. There are any number of reasons why a landlord may need to enter the unit: for maintenance purposes or to show the unit to a prospective tenant are two examples. In some states, the landlord does not even need permission to show the place to a possible tenant; only reasonable notice of intent to do so is necessary.

2. *To make repairs:* Most states allow the landlord to enter the unit without permission to make necessary repairs. Normally, all a landlord is required to do is give reasonable notice. It is good practice to give notice in writing and to keep a copy of the notice in your files. *You never know when such proof will come in handy.* After proper notice has been given, a tenant cannot legally deny access to the landlord.

3. *In an emergency:* In a real emergency, such as a fire, burglary, or medical crisis, the landlord can enter the unit immediately, without notice and without permission.

If you have given proper notice or made a proper request for entry and your tenant unreasonably refuses to let you in, you still can enter without the tenant's express authorization. It is your property, and the law recognizes that fact. Again, be sure to have put your request in writing. If forced to enter a unit after a tenant has denied you permission to enter, it is smart to bring along a witness when you do enter. After you have entered and done what you needed to do, and if your agreement is a month-to-month one, simply give thirty days' notice to terminate the tenancy and get rid of the problem tenant.

THE RIGHT TO CHANGE RENTAL AGREEMENT TERMS. Whether a landlord can change the terms of the agreement depends upon the agreement. A fixed-term lease (normally, but not always, for a year) cannot be changed. The terms of the agreement—rent, amount of security deposit, etc.—are, in fact, fixed while the lease is in effect. Once the lease ends and the tenancy terminates, a landlord is free to change the lease terms.

Unlike a fixed-term lease, most aspects of a month-to-month rental agreement are subject to modification. The landlord is free to change the terms as long as he adheres to proper notification requirements (usually thirty days). Provided that the change is legal, almost any alteration is permissible. A tenant can be told that pets will no longer be allowed, that rent will be raised, or that garbage fees will be assessed. If a tenant is unhappy with a proposed modification of the terms of the agreement, he or she can move.

The Important Legal Concept to Remember: Do not ever forget that it is the landlord who owns the property and that law was created to protect property rights. While tenants today have many rights, none trumps the rights of the property owner.

13

THE DUTY TO MAINTAIN AND REPAIR THE PREMISES

The duty to maintain
The duty to repair necessities
What the landlord does not have to do
Renter's insurance

THE DUTY TO MAINTAIN. As discussed in detail in Chapter 6, "The Implied Warranty of Habitability," every tenant has a right to a habitable home. This right creates a corresponding duty on the part of the landlord to provide and maintain a clean and safe dwelling for the tenant. While this right to a habitable home is implied in every rental agreement, most states have enacted housing and health codes that delineate exactly what a tenant should expect and what a landlord must provide.

In most states a landlord has a responsibility to provide and maintain running hot and cold water, heat, plumbing, a structurally sound building, a dwelling that is free from rodent or insect infestations, and clean and safe common areas—garbage facilities, lobbies, elevators, meeting rooms. These items are the duty of the landlord alone. A lease or rental agreement that attempts to put responsibility for these things on the tenant is illegal and unenforceable.

THE DUTY TO REPAIR NECESSITIES. The upshot of this duty to provide habitable premises is that the landlord is equally responsible for the repair of these items. If any are in need of repair after the tenant moves in, it is the landlord's responsibility to fix them.

A landlord must know about the problem before it can be fixed. Once the tenant has made the landlord aware of the problem, it should be fixed quickly. The tenant must cooperate and allow the landlord into the premises to fix the problem. If he does not, the landlord should give the tenant notice that he will enter the unit without permission, give a time and date for the entry, and then come in and fix the problem.

A landlord who fails to keep the dwelling in good repair should expect a timely visit from local housing authorities or the health department. A savvy unhappy tenant is usually not reticent to turn in a scofflaw landlord. Most building inspectors have the right to fine a landlord whose property is below statutory standards. Some communities even give building inspectors the power to close down a building that is in violation of safe housing laws.

Besides repairing necessities, in many cases a landlord has a responsibility to repair other, nonnecessity items that break due to normal wear and tear. For instance, if a faucet starts leaking, it is the landlord's job to repair it. The reason is that a tenancy is based upon a contract. The landlord's end of that deal is essentially that he will provide a nice place for his tenant to live. Therefore, a tenant whose paint finally fades after living in an apartment for many years probably has a right to have the place repainted. Normal wear and tear is the landlord's responsibility.

WHAT THE LANDLORD DOES NOT HAVE TO DO. While landlords have a duty to fix problems that threaten the habitability of the home and items that break due to normal wear and tear, they are not required to do more. Landlords certainly are not required to fix problems created by tenants or their guests.

Furthermore, landlords are not liable for criminal acts that could not be anticipated.

Patty rented a nice house in a quiet neighborhood from her landlord, Stan. The house had a garage that had been converted into a studio, so Patty parked her car on the street every night. One morning she came out to go to work and found that her car had been vandalized; the stereo was missing and the driver's side window had been smashed. Stan is not responsible for Patty's loss.

While landlords do have a responsibility to keep the dwellings they rent safe (see next chapter), they are not insurers; landlords are not, and cannot be expected to be, responsible for criminal acts they cannot anticipate. And in most cases, a landowner's insurance policy will not cover such a loss.

Landlords are also not required to replace the personal property of a tenant if the tenant's property was destroyed by what the law calls "an act of God." Storms, hurricanes, tornadoes, earthquakes, floods, and the like are not, despite what some tenants may think, a landlord's responsibility.

For example, if the pipes in a house freeze and then burst one December night, a landlord is not responsible for any damage to the personal property that a tenant may suffer. Yes, the landlord must repair the unit and make it livable again, but the cost of property replacement and new lodgings while the place is being repaired is the tenant's responsibility.

RENTER'S INSURANCE. Because of this, it is a very good idea for tenants to buy renter's insurance. The cost is really quite minimal, and the dividends can be huge. The policy would cover and replace all the belongings of the tenant that are damaged or destroyed due to an act of God, as well as the court costs and legal fees should the tenant ever get sued.

Jim's teenage son was practicing target shooting in the back-yard one afternoon when he accidentally hit the neighbor's prize horse. Jim's renter's insurance picked up the cost of hiring a lawyer as well as the $5,000 settlement.

If you own a lot of personal property, then a renter's policy is a necessity. Note that these policies vary greatly. If you live in a hurricane area, the policy may not pay for hurricane damage. For a small extra charge, the policy could cover expensive computers or family heirlooms. So, check with a good insurance agent and make sure that you buy the kind of policy that will cover any realistic possible loss.

The Important Legal Concept to Remember: Inside the rental, landlords are responsible for habitability and normal wear and tear, but nothing more. Renters are strongly advised to buy renter's insurance.

14

THE LANDLORD'S LIABILITY FOR CONDITIONS ON THE PREMISES

Common areas under the landlord's control

Negligent repairs

Crime

The need for insurance

Outside the four walls of the unit, landlords have other obligations. These responsibilities revolve around a general duty to keep the entire building safe and in good repair for the tenants. What a prudent landlord needs to understand is that if he fails in these broader responsibilities, the potential financial liability is hefty indeed.

COMMON AREAS UNDER THE LANDLORD'S CONTROL. It is the landlord's job to maintain, repair, and keep safe the common areas in a multiunit dwelling. Common areas are places under the control of the landlord and not any one tenant. Common areas include hallways, entryways, lobbies, stairs, elevators, yards, porches, meeting rooms, and any other area designated for the use and benefit of tenants.

The Bellvue apartments had a playground area for the children. After many years of use, the swing broke. In fact, the entire playground needed to be refurbished. The management tried to assess a fee on all tenants for the repair of the area. The tenants refused to pay, citing the rule that common areas are the landlord's responsibility. The tenants prevailed.

If a landlord fails to keep these common areas in good repair, *and* if a tenant is injured as a result of the landlord's omission, then the landlord will likely be held legally liable for any injuries suffered by the tenant.

Even though the management of the Bellvue apartments knew of the broken swing, it did nothing to warn its tenants of the problem. Unfortunately, before it was fixed, five-year-old Michela climbed on the swing and started to play. When the seat collapsed, Michela fell and broke her leg. The Bellvue's insurance company settled the claim for $30,000.

Almost any injury that can be traced back to a landlord's act, or failure to act, can constitute liability. In the language of the law, this is called a **tort**—a harm caused by another. In everyday language, this is called a personal injury. A broken stairway causing an injury, a defective electrical box causing a fire, or a rotted ceiling that collapses, harming someone, are all examples of a landlord's possible **negligence**.

NEGLIGENT REPAIRS. Landlords must keep common areas safe. That is the rule. That means that they must repair whatever is wrong with these areas—whether or not it applies to habitability—and that such repairs must be done properly. Negligent repairs are as much a source of liability as the original problem.

After the swing broke, the Bellvue hired a handyman to fix it. Instead of bolting the swing's seat back onto the chain, the handyman merely tacked it back on with an ill-fitting screw. Any injury resulting from his shoddy work would be the Bellvue's responsibility.

These responsibilities—to keep the complex in good repair and to fix any problems promptly and properly—should not be underestimated. Failing to live up to these responsibilities could result in a damage award to a tenant ranging into the *hundreds of thousands of dollars*. The owner of a duplex could easily lose his building if he is found liable in a personal-injury suit resulting from his negligence or that of his employees.

The question a judge will ask if you are ever in the unenviable position of having to defend a personal-injury suit is "Did this landlord act like a reasonable and prudent landlord under the circumstances?" This question is called the reasonable-person test. As a broad but useful generalization, a landlord who is said to have acted like a prudent, reasonable landlord would have under the same or similar circumstances will not be found to have been negligent. A landlord who is said to have acted unreasonable, either by omission or commission, will be held liable for a tenant's injuries.

There are many things a landlord can do to act reasonably and thereby to minimize his potential for liability. Have frequent inspections. Let your tenants know that you want to be notified as soon as possible of any problem. Post appropriate warning signs. Anything you can do to identify and rectify a potential problem will go a long way to help exonerate you should the unfortunate need ever arise. *You cannot be too cautious.*

CRIME. Another area landlords need to be concerned with is with regard to crime. Dwellings obviously need to be outfitted with locks (and probably deadbolts, to be "reasonable"), windows should have security features, although providing a security alarm is probably not necessary. Many localities have specific requirements regarding security, and it is best to find out what they are in your area.

In any case, the key again is to behave reasonably and do what a prudent landlord would do given the likelihood of crime in your complex. In higher crime areas, the landlord's duty increases correspondingly. While no landlord can guarantee total safety, what he must do is what would be reasonable under the circumstances.

A local gang of thugs had been hanging out around the Bellvue apartments for a month. Although the management knew about it, they did nothing to stop it. One of the residents was finally mugged, and she sued the Bellvue. The court found in favor of the resident. The court noted that the reasonable thing for the complex to have done under the circumstances would have been to hire a security guard for the building.

Almost anything that contributes to crime can be a possible cause for liability, such as inadequate lighting, a lack of security gates, or no security guards. While no landlord can insure against crime, he can and should take every possible precaution within the bounds of reason and economic reality to ensure that his tenants are as safe as can be expected.

THE NEED FOR INSURANCE. What with tenants who are willing to sue over almost any perceived problem and personal injury lawyers only too willing to take their cases, the landlord's potential for liability is great.

In order to minimize this risk, financially speaking, landlords should have plenty of insurance. **Comprehensive General Liability Insurance** (or CGL) is an insurance policy that serves two purposes. First, if you are sued, the policy will pay for the cost of the defense. If you have ever had to hire an attorney, you do not need to be told how helpful this aspect of the policy would be.

Second, if you are found liable, the policy will pay the damage award (in most cases) up to the policy limits. But think about that. If you have a policy with $100,000 in coverage and you get hit with a damage award for $300,000, then it is you, the landlord, who will be stuck paying the other $200,000. If your property is worth that much, you could lose it. That is why, although CGL coverage is not inexpensive, you should buy as much as you can afford. Liability insurance is a necessity for any landlord.

The Important Legal Concept to Remember: Be overly cautious. Inspect often. Fix problems properly and quickly. Get plenty of insurance.

15

LANDLORD REMEDIES I: PROHIBITED REMEDIES

Retaliatory evictions and rent increases
Preventing a retaliation allegation
Self-help evictions
Lockouts, seizures, and utility shutoffs

Almost all states have enacted laws that delineate exactly what actions a landlord can take against a problematic tenant. Such statutes can generally be divided into two sections: prohibited actions and permissible actions. Prohibited actions are explained here. Permissible actions are dealt with in the next chapter.

The gist of all prohibited-action statutes is that landlords cannot engage in **self-help**; they must follow the rule of law in order to rid themselves of an unwanted tenant.

RETALIATORY EVICTIONS AND RENT INCREASES. A landlord who has a tenant who constantly calls the health department, seemingly without reason, may understandably want to rid himself of that tenant. But if that landlord attempts to evict his problem tenant, he will lose. If a landlord can point to nothing more than an overzealous tenant, a judge will throw the eviction out and award the tenant attorney fees and costs.

A landlord cannot retaliate against a tenant who chooses to

enforce his legal rights. He cannot raise a tenant's rent for join-
ing a tenants' union. He cannot evict a tenant for complaining
to housing authorities. He cannot shut off the utilities of a tenant who is late with his rent. He cannot illegally retaliate.

Yet, while retaliatory evictions are illegal, they do occur, and
are often successful. This is especially true when a tenant has a
month-to-month tenancy since it can be terminated on thirty
days' notice for no reason. After all, it is quite difficult to prove
that a landlord's intent was retaliatory when he can terminate
the agreement at any time anyway.

In order to rectify this abuse, many states have enacted "presumption of retaliation" laws. These laws state that when an
eviction fairly quickly follows a complaint or other legal action
on the part of the tenant, it is the *landlord's responsibility to prove
that the action was not retaliatory*. A tenant doesn't need to prove
anything; the law presumes the eviction was retaliatory and
the landlord must disprove it. Thus, all a tenant often needs to
do is to get a copy of his local presumption of retaliation statute
and bring it to court.

In contrast, a retaliatory eviction is easy to prove when you
have a year-long lease. In that case, a landlord essentially can
evict a tenant only if he stops paying rent or harms the property. Absent proof of that, any eviction following the use of a
legal remedy is likely retaliatory.

Retaliatory rent increases are equally illegal. If a landlord
has more than one unit, then proving retaliation is actually
quite easy. Unless the landlord wants to raise everyone's rent at
the same time (and he usually does not), then all the tenant
needs to show are two things. One, he must be able to prove
that he recently utilized a legal landlord-tenant remedy. Two, he
must show that his rent alone was increased when others' were
not. The tenant wins. The landlord is fined.

PREVENTING A RETALIATION ALLEGATION. Here is how a landlord can avoid a false (or true) charge of retaliation:

- *Fix the problem:* If a tenant has a legitimate beef, resolve it quickly, and do not forget to document what you did. If the problem is imaginary, document that too.
- *Have a good reason to evict:* Landlords need a reason to evict a tenant, such as nonpayment of rent. Without good cause for the eviction, a retaliation charge will stick.
- *Wait:* If you do want to get rid of a tenant and your reason is in fact retaliatory, that is fine. It is still possible to avoid a retaliation allegation, *but only* if the tenant has a monthly rental agreement. If he does, then just wait a while. Wait five or six months, and then give notice to terminate the tenancy. It would also help if you could find some other, non-retaliatory reasons for the termination notice.

The same is true for retaliatory rent increases. Fix whatever problem the tenant complained about, wait a while, justify a rent increase, give plenty of notice of the proposed increase, and then raise his rent. He will leave.

SELF-HELP EVICTIONS. It should be no surprise that a landlord cannot evict his tenant without giving her proper notice and a day in court. It is illegal in almost every state for a landlord to enter the unit and physically evict a tenant and her belongings. Landlords simply must go through proper procedures. A landlord who resorts to illegal self-help evictions opens himself up to a nasty lawsuit in which he could end up owing his tenant a lot of money. That is a dumb landlord.

LOCKOUTS, SEIZURES, AND UTILITY SHUTOFFS. Even if they have done nothing to warrant retaliation, some tenants are just a pain. Some are more than a pain and are a liability risk. While you may be tempted, even justified, in wanting to take immediate action against such tenants, don't. *Self-help is illegal* and only gives a troublesome tenant ammunition.

One action that a landlord may contemplate is a **lockout:**

changing the locks while the tenant is gone, and either moving his stuff out or seizing his property. Lockouts are illegal in almost every state. Instead of locking out the problem, landlords must use the statutory eviction process. In fact, it is because evictions are now so streamlined that lockouts are illegal. Like it or not, agree or not, every tenant gets his day in court. Even if the lease states that lockouts are permissible, they are not. Such lease provisions are illegal and unenforceable.

A tenant facing an illegal lockout should take the following actions: First, call the police and tell them that your landlord is illegally trespassing on your property (which he is). The police may or may not act. The next step is to sue. A good attorney can get a court order permitting you back into the dwelling. A small claims action will allow you to recover monetary damages.

Just as lockouts are almost universally illegal, so are utility shutoffs. An angry landlord cannot shut off his tenant's utility service, period. Not paying the bill and causing the utilities to be shut off is also illegal.

The Important Legal Concept to Remember: Landlords cannot take the law into their own hands.

16

LANDLORD REMEDIES II: PERMISSIBLE REMEDIES

Working it out

Give notice to vacate or raise the rent

Notices to perform

Neither landlords nor tenants like evictions. Landlords lose rent and tenants lose homes. While sometimes necessary, there are many other options short of eviction that a landlord can try first to resolve conflicts with tenants.

WORKING IT OUT. It is a good policy, and certainly a less expensive one, to first try to resolve differences with your tenant informally.

Karen's tenant Bill had developed a bad habit of playing his saxophone around 10:00 P.M. most nights and she was getting a lot of complaints about him. Rather than simply giving Bill thirty days' notice, she went over to his apartment one night while he was playing. After visiting with him for a few minutes, she asked to hear him play. She complimented him on his style and then explained her problem to him. Karen told Bill that she liked him and wanted to keep him as a tenant, but that she really needed his help. Bill agreed that the music would stop by 9:00 P.M.

It does not matter whether the problem is late rent, loud noise, or parking in the wrong space, if you have kept an open-door policy, hopefully there is room to try one of these techniques:

- *Talking it out:* You might be surprised to find out that your tenants are more reasonable than you think. Most lawyers know that it is almost always smarter to negotiate amicably before getting nasty. Landlords should do the same. Be nice. Understand your tenant's dilemma. Try to find a fair solution.

- *The veiled threat:* If a reasonable compromise does not seem possible, then tell your tenant that you sure do not want to evict him, but you may have no choice. Sometimes all it takes is this kind of threat for a tenant to understand the seriousness of the matter and to then take action to correct the problem.

- *Friendly persuasion:* Here's a great trick: if eviction is a realistic alternative and therefore a credible threat, you can often avoid having to go through that process and get your tenant to move on his own accord by sweetening the pot. Tell your tenant that if you have to evict him, he will likely get no money back from his security deposit, but that if he voluntarily moves now, you will give him his entire deposit back, no questions asked.

GIVE NOTICE TO VACATE OR RAISE THE RENT. If these less formal techniques do not work and the tenant has a month-to-month tenancy, you can always change the terms of the agreement and see if that works. Raise rent or give thirty days' notice to vacate.

Raising rent often results in the tenant deciding to move on his own. The only thing to be cautious of is a possible retaliation allegation, if applicable. If it is, simply wait a few months before raising the rent. A more direct method is just to give the tenant notice to vacate. If your tenant refuses to move, you will then have to evict him.

NOTICES TO PERFORM. As a last resort, prior to filing an actual eviction action, you can always serve your tenant with a formal notice of your intent to take further action.

A Notice to Pay Rent or Quit is the first step in an eviction lawsuit. It tells the recalcitrant tenant either to pay the rent in a prescribed number of days or to leave the premises. The number of days varies, depending upon the state, but is usually quite short—three to five days is typical.

It is critical that the notice is filled out correctly, that the correct amount of past-due rent is stated, and that it is served properly. Since this notice begins the eviction process, it will be scrutinized by a judge to make sure it is complete and accurate, should it come to that. If it is not, then the entire eviction could be at jeopardy. If you do not know how to fill out the form correctly or calculate the past-due rent accurately or serve it properly, hire a lawyer or an eviction service. It will save you money in the long run.

Tenants are typically quite intimidated by Pay Rent or Quit Notices, and the need to actually continue the eviction process often dissipates after the tenant gets the notice. Many tenants are so terrified by the official-looking notice, which can be purchased at most office-supply or stationery stores, and so worried that they will be evicted the day after the notice expires (which is not true), they will beg, borrow, or steal the money needed to get caught up with rent.

If you really want to get your tenant's attention, here's a good idea: hire the local sheriff or an off-duty policeman to serve your tenant with the notice. You can rest assured that your tenant will not sleep well that night and that your past-due rent will be shortly forthcoming.

It is important to understand that a tenant does not have to leave at the expiration of the notice—that is not how the process works. You will still have to serve him with an eviction complaint and follow through with the eviction process. What this notice does do is tell your tenant that the jig is up. Remember, self-help is illegal. You must go through the proper channels to get rid of your problem tenant.

Another notice that may apply is the **Notice to Perform Covenant or Quit**. A covenant is a promise to do or not do something. Whereas a Notice to Pay Rent or Quit is used when tenants are late with rent, this notice is used when a tenant breaks some other type of promise in the lease or rental agreement.

> David rented a small flat from Louie. After living in the place for a few months, David had his girlfriend move in, even though his lease specifically stated that he was to be the only tenant in the unit. Louie did not approve of the arrangement, and immediately served David with a Notice to Perform Covenant or Quit. The notice specifically stated that David's girlfriend had to move out within three days or David would be evicted. David's girlfriend reluctantly moved.

> Similarly, if a tenant is keeping a pet when the lease forbids it, a Notice to Perform Covenant or Quit would be appropriate. These types of notices are very effective because tenants immediately realize that there will be dire consequences for continuing to break the rules.

The Important Legal Concept to Remember: The intimidation factor of a threatened eviction can often be the quickest and least expensive way for a landlord to get a tenant back in line.

TERMINATING
THE TENANCY

17

WHEN THE AGREEMENT ENDS

Month-to-month tenants who refuse to leave

Fixed-term lease tenants who refuse to leave

How to get out of paying last month's rent

How landlords can ensure that last month's rent is paid

Returning security deposits

How to get a security deposit back

Most tenancies end simply. The lease runs out and the tenant moves. Either party gives thirty days' notice and the tenant moves. But sometimes things are not so simple.

MONTH-TO-MONTH TENANTS WHO REFUSE TO LEAVE A monthly tenant who stays on after the term ends is called a **hold-over tenant**. Some of these tenants offer to pay rent again, while others stay on with no intent of ever paying rent again. When faced with a hold-over tenant, a landlord can either begin eviction proceedings or accept rent if proffered by the hold-over.

Landlords should be *extremely wary* of accepting rent again once a tenant holds over. Here is why: the tendering of rent is, in actuality, an offer to enter into a new rental contract. The acceptance of rent is an acceptance of that offer. Contracts are created by offer and acceptance. Once a hold-over tenant pays rent again, a *new rental contract* is created by operation of law. You are back at square one with your tenant.

> Shelly rented a duplex from Bob on a month-to-month basis. Shelly was not a great tenant, and Bob finally gave her thirty days' notice on August 1. On September 1, she failed to move out and officially became a hold-over tenant. A week later, when she realized that she would have a hard time finding a new place, Shelly sent Bob a check. Bob really needed the money and cashed the check. By cashing the check, Bob agreed to allow Shelly to stay. If he wanted to evict her now, he would have to wait until October 1 to give her a new thirty-day notice, and she would not have to leave until November 1.

By accepting Shelly's rent, Bob created a new rental agreement with her. This would be true for any landlord who accepts rent from a month-to-month tenant who holds over. It is generally a very bad idea, then, to take the money.

FIXED-TERM LEASE TENANTS WHO REFUSE TO LEAVE. A yearlong lease that starts on January 1 ends *automatically* on December 31 of that year. Neither tenant nor landlord needs to give any notice whatsoever.

Once the lease expires, there are four possible scenarios. The most common is that the tenant moves out, as he should. The second is that both parties decide to renew the lease, and rent begins again. The third is that the tenant holds over and does not pay rent. In that case, the landlord needs to evict him.

The fourth possibility is that the tenant holds over, offers to pay rent again, but signs no new lease. As in the case of a hold-over monthly tenant, a landlord can either accept or reject that offer of rent. If he accepts it, as in the case of Bob and Shelly above, a new rental agreement is created. However, instead of creating a new lease, as they did, the acceptance of rent from a lease-holding hold-over tenant creates a new *month-to-month* agreement. The lease expired, and the new rent does not revive it. All the new rent does is create a new monthly rental arrangement. So, be sure you want this tenant around for a while before you accept his rent after the term has expired.

If the landlord refuses the rent, then the tenant is still a hold-over. The landlord needs to evict him as he would any other tenant who does not pay rent.

HOW TO GET OUT OF PAYING LAST MONTH'S RENT. Whether you have a lease or a monthly rental arrangement, the thorny questions of security deposits and last month's rent are usually equally applicable. Often, a tenant will want to use the deposit as last month's rent and the landlord will not want him to. If the entire deposit is called a security deposit, the landlord is not obliged to apply any of it toward last month's rent. He can if he wants to, but he does not have to. It is the landlord's decision.

Do not be dismayed if you know that your landlord does not intend to apply a portion of your security deposit toward last month's rent. It is still possible to use part of that money for a last rental payment. Here's how: when you give notice, simply add to your written notice a few sentences telling your landlord that you will not be paying last month's rent and to apply the deposit (or a portion thereof) to rent. Of course your landlord will be unhappy, and may even give you a Notice to Pay Rent or Quit. That is fine. It will still take your landlord at least a month or so to evict you, so there is little he can actually do about it since you will be gone by the time you would have been evicted.

This trick works best if your deposit roughly equals your rent. Why? Your landlord is holding your money. Once she is mad at you, she will find every reason to keep the rest of your money. If your security deposit equals your last month's rent, then there will be nothing to keep.

HOW LANDLORDS CAN ENSURE THAT LAST MONTH'S RENT IS PAID. If a tenant decides not to pay rent the last month and tells his landlord to use the deposit instead, in reality there is not much a landlord can do. Eviction takes time. Try this instead:

> Amy owned a small house that she rented out on a month-to-month basis. It was her policy, as explained in her rental agreement, to allow tenants to move on *two weeks' notice.* Her tenant Anne lived in the house for a year. When Anne decided it was time to move, she had *already paid rent* that month. Since Anne knew that she needed to give Amy only two weeks' notice, she did not think to try to use her deposit as rent.

There is nothing illegal about requiring less time than required by law for tenants to give notice. If you require only two weeks' termination notice, then your tenant will likely have paid her rent by the time she gives notice. Try it, it works.

RETURNING SECURITY DEPOSITS. Landlords are required by law to itemize deductions and return security deposits promptly. In order to avoid confusion and ensure that they do not get sued in small claims court, landlords should follow these simple rules:

- *Require notice:* Require written notice of your tenant's intent to terminate the arrangement, and make sure that this requirement is part of the original rental agreement.
- *Offer guidelines:* Give tenants written guidelines describing what you require to refund a deposit in full. Have this notice explain that rent must be fully paid up to date, that the unit must be thoroughly cleaned, that all property must be removed, and that all keys need to be returned on the last day of the agreement.

- *Be honest:* Do not deduct for those items for which the tenant is not legally liable. Normal wear and tear is your responsibility; damage caused by the tenant is not.
- *Be timely:* Return deposits on time.

HOW TO GET A SECURITY DEPOSIT BACK. A tenant who wants her entire deposit back should do the following:

- Have your entire rent balance paid in full at the time you give notice.
- Pay your last month's rent on time.
- Give enough notice.
- Fix anything you broke.
- Leave the place spotless.
- Document the condition of the place (photographs, video-tape) after you have cleaned it.
- Return all keys promptly.

The Important Legal Concept to Remember: When the tenancy ends, tenants should leave and their deposits should be promptly returned. Failure by either party to live up to his obligations upon termination can be very costly.

18

GETTING OUT OF A
LEASE EARLY

Getting out early when the other side breaches the agreement

Surrender, abandonment, and mitigation

Assignments and sublets

GETTING OUT EARLY WHEN THE OTHER SIDE BREACHES THE AGREEMENT. A lease obligates both parties. The landlord is required to allow the tenant to possess the dwelling for the term of the lease and the tenant is obliged to pay rent for that amount of time.

Bill rented an apartment from Mark on a yearly lease basis at $500 per month. After eight months, Bill moved out without reason. Mark sued Bill for $2,000 ($500 x the 4 months remaining on the lease) and won.

If either party violates his obligations, he is in breach of the agreement. In that case, the *negatively affected* party has the right to simply call the whole deal off.

Rather than suing Bill, Mark just wanted to find a new tenant as soon as possible. He therefore terminated the lease and found someone else to rent the unit. Bill owed Mark no extra money.

Tenants too can terminate the lease if the landlord has substantially breached an obligation. Remember that landlords are obliged to deliver possession of a habitable unit and are required to ensure a tenant's quiet enjoyment of that dwelling. If a landlord fails in either of these duties, the tenant can void the remainder of the lease.

For example, when a landlord physically prevents a tenant from entering his home, he has committed what the law calls an actual eviction (although eviction here has a different meaning than the court procedure discussed earlier). Actual evictions allow tenants to move immediately, regardless of any binding lease. An example would be when a landlord padlocks the door of the unit if his tenant is a few days late with the rent. That is an actual eviction and the tardy tenant could simply end the lease and leave.

Even if a landlord is not foolish enough to actually evict a tenant, there are many other ways that a landlord can violate his obligations and negate the lease. Many of these breaches will result in what is known as a constructive eviction. Constructive evictions too permit the tenant to cancel the lease and leave.

Stacy's apartment was without heat for three months. She called her landlord several times, but to no avail. Finally, she moved out with six months remaining on her lease, claiming a constructive eviction. She was right.

Besides a lack of heat, other violations that may be cause for constructive eviction are

- *Breach of the warranty of habitability:* If a landlord continually fails to repair a major item—one that affects the habitability of the home—then a tenant can safely claim constructive eviction. Note, though, that the item must relate to the habitability of the home; a broken tile will not do. So too the landlord must be given a reasonable chance to fix the problem. A solitary phone call is insufficient.

· *Breach of the covenant of quiet enjoyment:* If a landlord continually interferes with a tenant's quiet enjoyment of the unit (by playing the tuba at all hours, for example), then the tenant can move due to a constructive eviction. Also, and this is an important point, if another tenant is too loud, *and the landlord has done nothing about it*, a tenant can claim a constructive eviction and terminate the lease.

Using constructive eviction to get out of a lease is a double-edged sword. The upside is that it is not difficult to make an argument that your landlord has violated some lease provision or implied covenant, and therefore you are justified in terminating the lease. The downside is that you had better be right. If you leave in the middle of the term and your landlord sues you for lost rent, you can be sure that a judge will carefully scrutinize your reasoning. If you are wrong, you will end up owing your ex-landlord a lot of back rent.

Finally, if the dwelling is destroyed, a tenant may terminate the lease and incur no further rent obligations. While that may be self-evident, the following may not be: if only part of the unit is destroyed, say, the garage, it still may be possible to terminate the entire lease. The key is to be able to prove that the garage was essential to your use of the dwelling, and that the lack of the garage materially impedes your enjoyment of the unit. If that can be proved, a tenant can get out of the lease. If it cannot, then the tenant is obliged to honor the agreement, despite the lack of a garage.

SURRENDER, ABANDONMENT, AND MITIGATION. Another way for a lease to end early is for the tenant to move out and give the unit back to the landlord, regardless of any breaches of the agreement. If this is done with the landlord's consent, it is called **surrender**; if it is done without it, it is called **abandonment**.

A surrender occurs when both parties agree to end the lease early and release each other from any further obligations. A surrender is often in the best interests of both sides. For the landlord, it saves the likely expense of suing the tenant for unpaid rent. For the tenant, it precludes possibly having to pay any more rent. If one side wants out, surrender is often a good choice. To be effective, the surrender must be in writing.

Abandonment, on the other hand, occurs when the tenant vacates the premises without agreement or permission and defaults on payment of rent. In that case, the landlord has two options. He can either do nothing and sue, or "accept" the abandonment.

While doing nothing and suing for lost rent sounds nice, the truth is, financial danger lurks for the landlord who makes that choice, due to a legal axiom known as mitigation. Mitigation means that a party to a breached contract must do everything possible to minimize any future financial loss he may suffer. In the case of a breached lease, it means that a landlord is required, in most states, to try to re-lease the unit in a reasonable amount of time.

Leslie moved out of her leased home three months early and left the place spotless. Her landlord, Tim, knowing he was required to mitigate his damages, was able to find a new tenant in just two weeks. Instead of being liable for three months of lost rent, Leslie was responsible for only the two weeks of lost rent incurred by Tim.

Even if it takes a landlord some time to repair, clean, and rent the unit again, he still will likely have to sue his tenant before he sees any of the back rent. And even then, the tenant may unfortunately be "judgment proof." Judgment proof is a term that brings tears to the eyes of lawyers and landlords alike. It means that even if found legally liable, the defendant does not have enough money or assets to pay the judgment (i.e., the court order to pay the amount due). A judgment that cannot be collected is a judgment that is worthless. Thus, suing for lost rent is not as easy as it sounds.

The other option, while not as emotionally satisfying as "suing the bastard," is sometimes the best one. That is to accept the abandonment and attempt to re-let the unit as soon as it is feasible to do so. In light of the duty to mitigate, and the cost and difficulty in obtaining and collecting a judgment, accepting and rerenting is often the most cost-effective solution.

ASSIGNMENTS AND SUBLETS. These are two final ways for a tenant to get out of a lease obligation before the lease ends, and without the baggage or risks associated with many of the options above. An assignment or a sublet allows someone else to take the tenant's place and finish the obligation for him.

If you are the tenant, an assignment is the better way to go. The reason is that an assignment allows the new party to take over a tenant's lease obligations completely. Basically, an assignment means that the new tenant's name will be written into the lease, the old tenant's name will be taken off the lease, and the old tenant's security deposit will be returned. All of the old tenant's legal obligations under the contract cease. If the new tenant defaults on rent, the landlord *cannot* come after the old tenant. To be valid, the assignment must be in writing.

Sublets are a bit different than assignments, and have substantially different legal consequences, even though they look the same. Both allow someone new to come in and live in the unit instead of the original tenant. However, whereas an assignment permits the original tenant to legally evade further obligations under the lease, that is not true of a sublet.

The key legal aspect of a sublet is that the original tenant *remains legally liable* to the landlord for all obligations under the lease. If the new tenant defaults on rent, it is the *original tenant* who is legally liable to the landlord. It is, therefore, a risky proposition for a tenant to sublet his unit. The original tenant gets none of the benefits of the lease (a place to live), yet still has all of the responsibilities. Accordingly, sublets are best used when a tenant may be gone for only a short period of time (say, for two months over the summer).

If you do sublet, realize that it is an agreement between the tenants only. Although the original tenant may need her landlord's consent to bring the new tenant in, the **sublease** agreement itself really has nothing to do with the landlord.

David had a great apartment overlooking the beach. When he got a job requiring a lot of travel, he decided to sublet his place. His sublessee, Steve, agreed that he would move in, pay rent, and vacate the place for a week every other month or so when David was back in town. This worked for six months. When Steve left the last time, David decided not to leave again. Steve was out of luck.

Almost all leases require the landlord's permission before a tenant assigns or sublets the lease to someone new. Normally, a landlord cannot "unreasonably" withhold his approval. Unfortunately, since determining what is reasonable is what makes lawyers rich, an uncooperative landlord can often withhold approval without repercussion.

Here is a trick that may get your landlord to approve your proposed transfer: find someone who is willing to accept the assignment or sublet and who would be willing to extend the length of the current lease. One reason landlords like leases is that they give a level of security—landlords know that the place is rented and will be until the end of the term. They do not have to think about cleaning and renting it again. Finding a new tenant who will extend the lease length dovetails with a landlord's desire to keep the place rented.

The Important Legal Concept to Remember: There are many ways to get out of a lease before it ends, although some are better than others. The best of all possible options is an assignment.

LAWSUITS

EVICTION LAWSUITS

Causes for eviction
The process
Trial
Eviction

CAUSES FOR EVICTION. Evictions occur after a tenant has been asked to move out and has refused to do so. With a month-to-month tenancy, a landlord ostensibly needs no reason to give thirty days' notice, since, by the very terms of the arrangement, either party can terminate the agreement on thirty days' notice. It is when a tenant has not moved on the thirty-first day that an eviction lawsuit is necessary. Eviction is a process that utilizes the assistance of the courts to put the landlord back in possession of the dwelling.

Clarence rented an apartment from Bruce and had a year-long lease. Bruce wanted to rent the unit to his brother, and therefore gave Clarence thirty days' notice to vacate. Since Clarence had a lease, and since he knew that Bruce could not legally give him thirty days' notice, Clarence did nothing. When Bruce tried to evict Clarence, the judge threw the case out of court and made Bruce pay all of Clarence's legal bills.

The critical question to be answered by the courts is whether a landlord has a justifiable reason to possess the property again.

If a tenant has an ongoing lease and has done nothing wrong, a landlord has no right to possess the property until the lease is up. A landlord like Bruce will lose his eviction lawsuit because a court will decide that he has no justifiable reason to gain possession of the property again. His tenant did nothing wrong.

So, the issue is this: has the tenant given the landlord a legally justifiable reason for taking the property back? A tenant who has properly withheld a portion of her rent to fix a broken shower has not given her landlord just cause for an eviction. A tenant who has withheld a portion of her rent because she thinks her landlord charges too much rent has in fact given her landlord just cause for eviction. In the former case, the law allows for repair and deduct. In the latter, there is no right to unilateral, unjustifiable rent withholding. Is the law on your side? That is the question.

Just cause for terminating a tenancy includes all of the following: nonpayment of rent, expiration of the term, the tenant is disturbing other tenants, the tenant has damaged the property, the tenant has violated a term of the agreement (e.g., a no-pets clause), or the tenant is breaking the law in the unit. Any one of these would likely result in a victory for the landlord.

THE PROCESS. Once it has been established that a landlord has a valid reason to evict a tenant, usually, but not necessarily, for nonpayment of rent, he does so by initiating a lawsuit, usually called an **unlawful detainer** or a **forcible entry and detainer** action. Unlawful detainer actions are expedited court processes, typically taking anywhere from *one week to two months, from start to finish.*

Evicting someone is not the type of thing one should attempt to do without the assistance of a professional. Eviction services run by **paralegals** are available at a small fee, but you get what you pay for. Paralegals are not attorneys and cannot give legal advice. They also cannot go to court with you. If you can afford it, it is much smarter to hire an attorney.

The eviction begins when the landlord, or his attorney, files a **complaint** against the tenant. The complaint identifies the **parties**, states the reasons for the action, and requests that the tenant be evicted.

After the complaint is filed (by the party called the plaintiff), it must be **served**, along with the **summons**, on the tenant. Although each state has different rules, service is usually accomplished by either (1) personal delivery by a sheriff or registered process server, (2) tacking the summons and complaint to the door of the rental, or (3) certified mail. Since improper service constitutes grounds to dispute the eviction, *be sure the tenant is served properly.*

In an unlawful detainer action, the person being sued (named as the **defendant**) has a very short amount of time to file a response with the court and the other side, and some states do not even require a formal response. Tenants are advised to read the summons carefully; it will state whether a formal written response is required, and, if so, by when. If a written response is required and the tenant fails to respond in time, then the landlord can save the time and expense of a trial by filing for a **default** judgment. By defaulting, a tenant forfeits his right to go to trial. The landlord wins automatically.

If the tenant does respond to the suit, it will go to trial in a very short amount of time. A landlord may find his tenant trying to forestall an eviction trial, and thereby stay in the unit even longer, by filing some sort of **motion** with the court (see next chapter). If a landlord has acted properly, then such a motion is nothing but a delaying tactic.

TRIAL. Eviction trials vary depending on state law. Some states allow for jury trials, others do not. Some eviction trials are notoriously quick, lasting no more than fifteen minutes or so; others may last half a day. The issues are whether the landlord acted properly, filed suit properly, gave notice and served the tenant properly, and whether he has a right to retake the unit. Similarly, the judge will want to know why the tenant did whatever he did, and whether he had any justification for his actions or inactions.

Again, if you can afford an attorney, it is best to hire one. Trials are complicated, and if you do not know what you are doing, the judge will quickly stop you. Judges do not suffer fools lightly.

Whether or not you have an attorney, you still must act appropriately in court. How you behave will have a significant impact on the outcome of your trial. Dress nicely. Exercise decorum and self-restraint. Do not overreact. Do not argue with your tenant or landlord. Present yourself well, and speak only to the judge. Do not chew gum. Be on time. Do not whisper. Be respectful.

The key to being believed when testifying is to be honest. Your testimony must be credible, make sense, and have the ring of truth to it. Judges instinctively know when someone is lying. Speak up. Be calm. Do not memorize answers. Listen to the question, and answer only the question asked. If you do not understand a question, ask for it to be repeated. Do not avoid the truth, even though it may be unflattering. Be clear, concise, and honest.

In order to win, not only must you act appropriately but you must also have the law on your side. If you are a tenant and have not paid your rent, you had better have a legal justification for your inaction, such as repairing and deducting. You also need to come to court well organized, with documents and witnesses who can help you prove your case. The party who comes in unorganized, ranting and raving, with no proof, loses.

EVICTION. Assuming, not illogically, that the landlord won the eviction trial, the tenant must usually move within a matter of days. In some states, tenants have one day to move; in others, twenty-one. California, for example, gives a tenant five days to leave after trial.

Tenants should leave peacefully before the deadline. If by the deadline they are not gone, the police will physically evict them. Their property will be immediately removed. Again, it is best to avoid this ugly scene and just move before the deadline.

The Important Legal Concept to Remember: Landlords usually win eviction lawsuits because they know what they are doing and have done it many times. Unless a tenant truly has a reason that can stand up in court, it is best for everyone concerned if the tenant just moves out when served with the suit.

20

DEFENDING AN
EVICTION LAWSUIT

Defending against an eviction
Other Options

It is not easy for a tenant to defend an eviction action. Landlords usually have more resources (i.e., money and lawyers),
as well as a justifiable reason for bringing the suit. Many tenants
do not even bother to show up for the trial, knowing that the
outcome is almost predetermined.

Yet it need not be so. There are two different possible avenues
a tenant can take once served with an eviction complaint. The
first option is to assert a legitimate affirmative defense. An affirmative defense is a defense that, if applicable to you and can be
proved, will enable you to win in court and stay in the dwelling.
The second option is to utilize a legally permissible procedural
motion, which may also buy you some time.

The first course of action—asserting an affirmative defense—
should be used if you really believe that you have done nothing
wrong and should not be evicted. The second option—using
legal procedure—is used when you suspect that your landlord
has a good reason to evict you, but also think that he may have
improperly handled the eviction proceeding. A positive by-
product of filing a procedural motion is that it may allow you
to stay in the unit a bit longer, if that is your desire.

DEFENDING AGAINST AN EVICTION. If you believe that the landlord should not be evicting you, the first thing to consider is whether you want to hire an attorney. It is possible to get very inexpensive legal help. Try the following:

- *Yellow Pages:* Look under "Legal Aid," "Legal Services," or "Legal Clinics." All of these are headings for nonprofit groups that specialize in helping poor people out of legal pickles.
- *Law schools:* Most law schools have clinics, run by attorneys, that teach law students how to become lawyers. Assisting in landlord-tenant disputes is often their specialty.
- *Local bar associations:* A **bar association** is an organization of lawyers found on local, state, and national levels. Many have voluntary legal-assistance programs. Call the local bar association in your city.

Next, whether or not you have an attorney, you need to decide which defenses to assert. These defenses are asserted both as part of your "response" to the complaint (if so required in your state) and at trial. They are the basis for your argument that you should be allowed to stay in the unit. There are many such defenses, depending upon the reason for the eviction. For example:

- *For nonpayment of rent:* If your landlord is evicting you for nonpayment of rent, the first and obviously best defense would be to be able to prove that it was, in fact, paid. Absent that possibility, there still are several viable defenses. Asserting and proving that your landlord breached the warranty of either habitability or quiet enjoyment would also work. Why? Because the law allows you to withhold rent when your landlord has breached these implied promises.
  Another possible defense is that your landlord failed to perform other obligations under the agreement. For exam-

ple, if your landlord failed to keep the common areas clean and safe. In essence, you need to be able to prove that you had a legally justifiable reason for not paying rent. Excuses, unjustifiable reasons, or an inability to pay will not suffice.

· *For nonpayment of a rent increase:* If you refused to pay a rent increase, a particularly good defense, if it can be proven, is that the increase was either retaliatory or discriminatory. Asserting these defenses are particularly effective as they turn the tables; your landlord will be on the defensive and will have to prove that the increase was not made for an improper purpose. In legal parlance, these defenses shift the burden of proof from you to your landlord. Remember that merely asserting retaliation will not do; you must be able to prove retaliation or discrimination with witnesses or documents, preferably both.

Another defense to a rent increase is that you were not given proper notice of the increase. A tenant with a month-to-month tenancy deserves at least thirty days' notice of the increase. Anything less is improper and therefore solid grounds to defend the action.

· *For any other reason:* There are a variety of other reasons that a landlord may assert as reason for eviction. Almost all of the defenses listed above apply equally to many of these causes. For example, say your landlord is evicting you because he says you had a boyfriend move in, in violation of the lease. Proving that he did not actually move in, but merely spent the night sometimes, would be quite effective. It would be especially helpful if you could get some neighbors to testify to that effect. Be creative and tell the truth.

These, then, are your basic defenses: rent *was* paid; retaliation or discrimination; the landlord failed to perform an obligation, thereby causing you to withhold rent; breach of the warranty of either habitability or quiet enjoyment; use of repair and deduct; improper notice of a change in the terms of the tenancy; or a defense on the merits (e.g., you never had a pet—you were only pet-sitting for a friend for a few weeks). If any of these apply to you and you can prove it, then by all means defend yourself.

OTHER OPTIONS. If none of these defenses applies to you and you have no real justification for doing whatever it is your landlord is angry about, it is better just to move. The only reason to stay would be if you think that the eviction was handled improperly. If so, use one of the options below. While they will not save you, they may at least buy you some time.

The first tactic is to file a motion with the court. Previously, it was stated that a tenant sometimes needs to file a response to the complaint, normally *within a matter of days of service of the complaint*. Usually this response is an **answer**—a document that essentially denies that the tenant did anything wrong. Yet an answer is not the only answer. There are two other possible responses that you can file instead. It is important to understand that these responses, called motions, *must be filed in good faith*. Filing a frivolous motion (one that cannot be supported by any facts) is a sure way to get monetarily sanctioned by the court. As each of the two motions listed below serves a very specific purpose, be sure that your case has similar facts before filing either one.

The first is something called a **motion to quash**. A motion to quash is used when you believe that you were not served correctly. Service of the eviction lawsuit normally must be accomplished by personal delivery, certified or first-class mail, or tacking the complaint on your door. If your landlord never served you with the summons and complaint personally, but just shoved the documents under the door while you were gone, then a motion to quash would be appropriate.

Realize that a motion to quash is a fairly technical motion. It is a good idea to go down to your local courthouse and get a copy of one, or to find a book that has one. Copy it, fill in your facts, file it with the court, and serve it on your landlord. If the judge determines that you were not served legally, then your landlord will need to start the eviction process all over.

The other possible motion to file instead of an answer is something called a **demurrer**. A demurrer tells the court that your landlord has no *legal* justification for the eviction.

Brian had a year-long lease with his landlord, Jeff. Halfway through, Jeff served Brian with a thirty-day notice to vacate. Brian refused to move, noting that he had a lease. When Jeff then served Brian with an eviction complaint, Brian filed a demurrer, arguing that it is legally impossible to evict someone on thirty days' notice when he has a lease. The judge agreed, and Brian stayed in his home.

Whether you should file a demurrer really depends upon the facts of your case. Grounds include improper notice of a change in the tenancy or termination of the tenancy, improper use of a Notice to Perform Covenant or Quit, and filing the complaint too soon, among others.

If you are contemplating a demurrer, understand that you are entering a very, very technical area of the law. It is really an area that only lawyers should tread. But if you want to file one and you do not have an attorney, the first thing to know is that a demurrer tests the *legal* sufficiency of the case, not its *factual* sufficiency. A demurrer is not the place to say that your landlord is a slumlord. That is a factual issue. It is the place to say that he filed suit against you before ever giving you a Notice to Pay Rent or Quit, as he is legally obliged to do. Again, get a copy of a demurrer to use as a prototype, and change the facts accordingly. As a demurrer is so specialized, do not expect to win.

Another option, and one that might buy you some time, is to ask for a **continuance.** This is made before the trial, by filing a written request with the court. A continuance is granted only for good cause—an important witness will be out of town or you cannot get off from work that day, for example. If granted, this might give you another two weeks.

Another possible way to delay moving is to cut a deal with your landlord prior to trial. Your landlord really does not want to go to trial either, surprisingly enough. Trials cost him money in legal fees and continued lost rent. They are also risky; your landlord could possibly lose.

Your landlord may be willing to work with you if you can assure him that you will pay him what you owe him and will move out on a certain date. Especially if you let your landlord know that you have the procedural tricks outlined above up your sleeve, he may be far more likely to negotiate with you. Remember, you are still in possession of his property and are therefore negotiating out of a position of strength. Cut a good deal and get out already.

The Important Legal Concept to Remember: Tenants who know they deserve to be evicted should save their money and move out before trial. Those who feel justified in fighting the suit must be prepared to prove to a judge that their actions were legally justified.

21

SMALL CLAIMS COURT

Lawsuits in general
Small claims or superior court?
Filing suit in small claims court
How to present your case

LAWSUITS IN GENERAL. There are many reasons why a land-lord or tenant may want to sue the other. Unpaid rent, an unre-turned security deposit, discrimination, injury—the list is probably endless. Often, the most pressing reason is emotion-al—one party is just so mad at the other that a lawsuit seems like the best way to get back at him. And it often is. And, it often is not.

When faced with a problem that cannot be solved in a man-ner to your liking, and you are determined to get a different result, then your only option is to sue the person or entity who is aggrieving you. For better or for worse, lawsuits are just about the only legal method society has developed to resolve such disputes.

There are distinct advantages to filing suit. First, it puts your foe on notice that you are not to be taken lightly. It tells him that you have been harmed and that you refuse to take it any-more. Suing someone also puts him on the defensive. Indeed, throughout the suit you will be known as the plaintiff and he will be known as the defendant.

Filing suit also will (eventually) allow a neutral third party—the judge—to decide who is right and who is wrong. If you are right and can convince the judge, then you will be financially rewarded for your troubles. Except in the rare cases when a restraining order or similar legal device is required, money is all the law offers.

Kelly nearly died when she went for a swim in the pool at her apartment complex and discovered that it had been overchlorinated. Throughout her long suit, she demanded a public apology from the management of her complex. She told the judge the same thing. The jury awarded her $10,000. She never did get that apology.

The law cannot heal a broken leg or mend a broken heart. It cannot bring back a dead parent or comfort a traumatized child. However crude, money is all the law has to offer.

SMALL CLAIMS OR SUPERIOR COURT? Once you have determined that you want or need to sue someone, the next question to answer is whether to bring your suit in small claims court or superior court.

For most landlord-tenant disputes arising out of unpaid rent or a security deposit that was not returned, small claims court is the way to go. Small claims court is an informal, inexpensive, expedited process that is designed to settle disputes over small amounts of money. In Vermont, the most you can sue for is $3,500. In California, the limit is $5,000. In Georgia, it's $5,000, and in South Dakota, the maximum judgment is $4,000. Each state is different.

If the money you feel you are owed exceeds these limits (for example, if you suffered a physical injury or were discriminated against), then you will need to bring suit in a superior court (depending upon where you live and where you file, such courts are also called district courts, county courts, municipal courts, courts of common pleas, and the like). Whereas small claims court is quick and inexpensive, just the opposite is true for superior court. Cases often take years and hiring an attorney is a necessity.

The old television show *People's Court* was nothing more than glorified small claims court. While some states allow you to hire an attorney to represent you, it is not necessary. In fact, one of the great advantages of small claims court is that you are able to represent yourself without having to resort to hiring expensive attorneys.

FILING SUIT IN SMALL CLAIMS COURT. Bringing an action in small claims court is easy. Simply go down to your local courthouse, fill out the appropriate forms, and pay the fee. It should be somewhere around fifty dollars. When the form asks why you are suing, write in "breach of contract" or whatever your reason is.

Do not sue for more than you are legally entitled. In the case of a security deposit that was not returned, a tenant is entitled to the amount of the deposit plus interest, and any possible fines. Time for missed work, baby-sitters, emotional distress, and the like, are normally not compensable and will only weaken a case. The same is true for back-rent lawsuits.

The court will probably mail the necessary notices to both parties, informing everyone of the date and time of the hearing. It usually takes less than three months to get into small claims court.

HOW TO PRESENT YOUR CASE. The key to winning in small claims court is the two P's: preparation and proof. You must be able to *prove* to the judge that what you are telling her is true and that your opponent's version of the facts is false. You do so by being *prepared*.

Preparation means that you are fully organized and ready to present your case before the judge in a short amount of time. It is safe to assume that you will have about ten minutes to tell the judge your side of the facts. In order to do so, you need to have already organized your case.

Have your witnesses prepared and ready to testify. Speak with them beforehand and let them know where and when court will be. Call them the day before your hearing and remind them of the court date. Be sure to make an outline of your case. Before you get to court, you also need to have made copies of all relevant receipts, letters, and other documents. Like a Boy Scout, be prepared.

Sam found a nice house for rent, filled out the application, and gave his new landlord, Larry, a $500 security deposit. Sam lived in the place for seven months before deciding to move. He gave Larry thirty days' notice. Before he left, Sam thoroughly cleaned the house. Because he had had many problems with Larry in the few months he lived there, Sam decided to take a few photographs of the place before he left. He also had his pal Ron walk through the unit with him before he returned the key. Predictably, Larry never returned Sam's security deposit, even after Sam wrote a demand letter.

Even more important than preparation, though, is proof. Sam must be able to prove that he is entitled to a return of his security deposit. If he had no pictures, evidence, or witnesses, and simply told the judge his version of the facts, he would likely lose. A landlord is a businessperson who owns real estate. In the legal world, that carries weight. Tenants are often seen as less responsible. In many cases a judge will likely side with a landlord if a tenant simply goes in with her word against his. That is a sad but true fact.

So, you need evidence. Have extra copies of your lease and demand letter ready. Pictures and a videotape are indispensable. Witnesses must show up on time and be ready to testify succinctly. If you don't have any evidence, you are wasting your time and money.

When you get your day in court, dress professionally. As the plaintiff, you will get to speak first. One thing your judge will not want to see is a lot of emotion. The law in these types of matters is fairly clear-cut. Hot tempers and hurt feelings carry little weight with judges. What does carry weight is a clear, simple explanation of why you are legally entitled to money. Organize your case something like this:

1. *Give a one- or two-sentence description of the dispute.* "I lived at 1800 Mariposa Lane for eight months. I gave my landlord, the defendant, Larry Brooks, a five-hundred-dollar deposit, and he refused to return it to me when I moved out." Show the judge the receipt for your deposit.

2. *Explain why you should get your money back.* " I left the unit in the exact same condition as I found it. In fact, it was probably cleaner when I left than when I moved in. I also paid all of my rent, and I can prove it, Your Honor."

3. *Prove it.* Show the judge whatever photographs you have. Have your witnesses testify that you did, in fact, leave the place clean and in good repair. Show any receipts or canceled checks you have to prove that all rent was paid. Show your demand letter. Explain that you tried to be reasonable.

After the plaintiff presents his case, the defendant will have a chance to give his version of the facts. Do not interrupt him, as you will get another chance to rebut whatever he says. Proper decorum is critical in a courtroom.

Do not be surprised if the defendant lies. People lie in court all the time, plaintiffs and defendants alike. If your landlord says that you broke the refrigerator, you must be able to prove that you did not. If your tenant says that he paid all of the back-due rent, be ready to prove otherwise. The side who can prove his version of the facts will win.

After the defendant has presented his case, the plaintiff will have one more chance to speak. The first thing to do is to rebut what the defendant said. Then explain again in an abbreviated form why you should win. *Do not* try to present your entire case again. You will be told to be quiet.

The judge may render a judgment right there, or he may tell you that it will come in the mail in a week. If you win, congratulations. If you lose, you may have a right to appeal, but then it starts to get costly. Be sure you are right before you appeal a loss.

The Important Legal Concept to Remember: You have a much better chance of winning your small claims case if you remember to use the two P's: preparation and proof. If you do, then you do not have to be bullied—a small claims judge can get your money back for you.

22

SUPERIOR COURT

WHY YOU SHOULD BE WARY OF LARGE LAWSUITS. If your problem is more complex, then suit will need to be filed in your local superior, district, or county court. Such courts are where disputes over large amounts of money are resolved. A superior court case is needed when, for example, a child was seriously injured due to a landlord's alleged negligence, or a tenant allegedly suffered discrimination.

A lot of consideration is needed before bringing such a suit. Unlike small claims cases, superior court cases are very lengthy, very time-consuming, and very expensive. So, before threatening a landlord or tenant with a big, fat lawsuit, you had better understand that these sorts of lawsuits are clumsy and lengthy, and emotionally and financially draining.

When you sue someone in a district court, it is called litigating a case. **Litigation** is war. In fact, in most law firms, the place where the lawyers keep exhibits, motions, and evidence, and where they prepare for trial, is called the "war room." What does that mean? It means you should expect that your opponent will do whatever is necessary to win—spend money, hire experts, locate evidence, and so on. You can rest assured that the other side will be just as willing as you are to say and do almost anything in order to win. Again, this is war.

Tenants especially need to be careful before they give an attorney a large **retainer** since, in most cases, landlords have more money than they do. As such, a landlord is normally better able to pursue or defend a case aggressively, and may eventually wear down the tenant to the point where the tenant simply can no longer financially afford to continue the suit. In most cases, the only time a tenant is on a level playing field is when he has an attorney who is doing the case on a **contingency** basis (see below).

Now, it is true that 95 percent of all cases settle. That does not mean, however, that 95 percent of all cases settle in the plaintiff's favor. Defendants countersue, and sometimes the settlement is in their favor. Sometimes the plaintiff simply quits; that too is a form of settlement. It is only when the defendant clearly harmed the plaintiff, *and* it can be proven, *and* the plaintiff can afford to go to trial, that a settlement will probably occur in the plaintiff's favor.

But what if things are not so clear? In that case, the suit *will* go to trial. Trial too is an inherently dangerous proposition. The problem there is that judges, by nature and law, do not take sides. Their job is to be independent, fair, objective, intelligent, rational, and law abiding. A judge may allow favorable evidence in, or she may not. While you may be positive that you will win, in the judge's mind your chances are at best fifty-fifty. The old legal axiom, learned the hard way by many a litigant, is *You never know what a judge or a jury will do.* Remember, one jury acquitted O. J. Simpson while another did not. You never know what a judge or jury will do.

Therefore, unless you are willing to commit fully the time and resources necessary to see the case to fruition, it is best simply to forget the suit, however difficult that may be.

So, now you heard the bad news, and, yes, there is some

good news. While litigation and trial are cumbersome undertakings, they are also worth it, *if you win*. Because if you win, you will likely win a substantial amount of money. And when you have been harmed, there is a lot of satisfaction in getting money from the one who harmed you. So, if you are prepared to take this arduous journey, read on.

FINDING A GOOD LAWYER. The first thing to do is to find a good attorney. The very best place to find one is from a satisfied customer. Word-of-mouth advertising will tell you far more about a lawyer than a dozen television commercials. If you know someone who has had success with a lawsuit recently, find out how she liked her attorney, how long the case took, whether the lawyer returned phone calls promptly, how much money she spent, and whether she was happy with the result.

Similarly, if you have a friend who is a lawyer, ask him, but do not hire him. There are more good lawyers than good friends around. If you do not know any attorneys, and don't know anyone who knows any, then finding one gets a bit more difficult. Try to stay away from any referral services aside from that sponsored by your local bar association. Other referral services, found in the phone book, usually have but one requirement of the attorneys they recommend—money. Any lawyer who pays the fee required by the referral service will probably be recommended by that service. The local bar association is an organization of local lawyers, grouped by practice area, who often have a referral service based upon expertise, not profit.

The final option is advertising. Almost all attorneys, good and bad alike, now advertise. If a Yellow Page or television ad catches your fancy and the lawyer practices in litigation, schedule an interview and go speak with him.

As indicated previously, if you are the potential plaintiff, it is best if you can find an attorney who will take the case on a contingency basis. Contingency means that the attorney will not ask for any money up front, but instead will take a percentage of any settlement or judgment—33 to 40 percent is typical. The added advantage is that you will quickly find out if your case has any merit. Contingency lawyers carefully review the facts of the dispute as they cannot afford to take a case that is not likely to succeed.

The one big drawback to contingency agreements is that they normally only work when there has been a personal injury. Attorneys do not usually accept contingency cases for other types of disputes. If you are in the unfortunate position of having to defend a suit, no attorney will take your case on contingency.

> Stuart had a three-year lease with his landlord. Eight months into the lease, Stuart's company decided to send him to Tokyo for a year. Stuart subleased his apartment to Abby, but never told his landlord. After Stuart left, his landlord found out about the sublease and evicted Abby. When he returned, Stuart found a stranger living in his flat and all of his possessions, worth in excess of $20,000, missing. After speaking with three different attorneys, Stuart gave up on the idea of suing his landlord since none of the lawyers would take the case on contingency and he could not afford the $5,000 retainer each required.

HOW THE CASE PROCEEDS. A lawsuit begins when one side files a complaint against the other. Typically, the defendant has thirty days to file an answer.

The next phase of the suit is spent conducting **discovery**. Discovery is the formal process that allows both sides to discover information from the other. How much property does the landlord actually own? Has this tenant filed similar lawsuits in the past? Was he really hurt, or is he faking it? Does the landlord have a history of discriminating? That is discovery.

The filing of the complaint and the response and the discovery process can take as short as a few months or as long as a few years. It depends upon the attitudes of the parties, the complexity of the issues, and the amount of money involved.

As a general rule, the more money there is at stake, the longer the case will likely take.

HOW THE CASE MAY END. Any lawsuit can end in one of four ways: (1) the parties agree to a settlement; (2) the parties cannot agree on anything and the case goes to trial; (3) either the plaintiff or the court dismisses the case (the defendant cannot dismiss a case); or (4) the defendant fails to answer the complaint and loses by default.

Settlement and trial are the most common outcomes. If one side clearly has harmed the other, then a settlement is more likely. Because taking a case all the way to trial is such an expensive proposition, a party that is obviously in the wrong will usually want to settle the case to avoid that expense.

It is when the issues and facts are more complex and liability is less clear that a case will go all the way to trial. You can expect that your case will take one to three years before it ever gets there.

TRIAL. There are essentially four parts to a trial: opening statements, the plaintiff's case, the defendant's case, and closing arguments.

Notice that a trial begins with an opening *statement* but ends with a closing *argument*. They are quite different. Argumentative interpretation of what happened in your case is reserved for the conclusion. The beginning of the trial is a chance for the plaintiff's attorney to tell the judge or jury what she intends to prove during the trial. The attorney will likely give a brief overview of the case and explain her theory of why her client should win. The defendant's attorney will then do the same.

After each side has given its opening statement, the plaintiff will present her version of the facts. The lawyer will call witnesses intended to back up the theory of the case. If the issue is discrimination, the plaintiff's lawyer will call witnesses who will show that the landlord has a history of discriminatory practices.

The most important witness in your case will be you. After being called to the stand, your lawyer will ask you a series of questions. This is called direct examination. You and your attorney should have gone over these questions many times; you should not be caught off guard by a question your attorney asks. Answer the questions directly and honestly.

In cross-examination, the opposing lawyer will attempt to discredit you and your testimony. He will be very aggressive, even hostile. Expect incidents in your past to come up that may cast doubt on your integrity. Also, expect facts to come up that contradict your testimony. Do not expect to be treated with much respect.

There are two important factors that determine how a judge will rule in a case—law and facts. Laws are subject to much interpretation, and each lawyer will, throughout the course of the trial, argue as to why a certain legal interpretation should apply to a certain set of facts. The bulk of the trial will be taken up with what happened during the tenancy—the facts of the case. When contradictory facts are introduced, it is up to the jury (or, if you have no jury, the judge) to decide who is telling the truth and what the real facts are.

After the plaintiff presents her case, the defendant will get a chance to do the same. Witnesses giving a very different interpretation of what happened will be called. Facts about the plaintiff that are unflattering will come out.

After all witnesses have been called, closing arguments are made. Although the members of the jury may have made up their minds by this point, these arguments are important. It is a chance for the lawyers to put forth their best interpretation of the case, as proven with the evidence presented. After both sides have concluded their arguments, the judge or jury will rule on the case.

The Important Legal Concept to Remember: Ever risky, lawsuits are nevertheless one of the only retribution options society offers to harmed individuals. If you have been injured and are willing to commit the necessary resources to see your case through, then sue. Don't say you weren't warned, though.

VI

APPENDICES

COMMON QUESTIONS
AND ANSWERS

Can a form lease or rental agreement be changed?
Yes. A form contract is still a contract. And, like all contracts, it takes two to tango. It is not called an agreement for nothing. Although a form contract looks imposing, it is easy to change. Simply agree with the other side as to the changes needed, strike out the offensive language or clause, and have both sides initial the change. That's it.

Do I have a right to inspect the unit before I move in?
No, you have no "right," per se, to do so. However, you certainly have every reason to want to have a thorough walk-through before signing any agreement so that any flaws in the dwelling can be noted. If your potential landlord refuses to let you inspect the particular unit you will be renting, you do not want it anyway

TENANT RIGHTS, DUTIES, AND SOLUTIONS

Can I change the unit after I move in?
It depends upon whether your lease or rental agreement forbids it. If it does, and you make changes anyway (paint, put up bookshelves, etc.), then you have breached the lease and can be evicted. If there is no clause preventing you from doing so, then you most certainly can make changes. Be aware, however, that you cannot decrease the value of the unit, and that if you make

fairly permanent changes, they will become the property of the landlord due to the doctrine of "fixtures."

Although my unit is rent-controlled, my landlord just raised my rent. What should I do?
Rent control is not the same as rent freezing—landlords can raise rent under the right circumstances. The first thing to do is to check the local rent-control ordinance or call the local rent-control board to see whether your landlord had a legal right to do what he did. If your landlord did raise your rent illegally, first try to work it out informally with him. If that fails, file a complaint with your rent-control board. If all else fails, hire a lawyer.

My landlord just told me that I cannot have my girlfriend spend the night anymore. Can he do that?
Probably not. It really depends upon how often she stays. Your landlord agreed to rent to you, not to you and her. If she has basically moved in, your landlord is right. If, however, she is there only a few nights a week, he is overstepping his ground. You have a right to be left alone in the quiet enjoyment of your own apartment. Your landlord cannot violate this right without also violating the law.

My landlord wants to sell the house I lease. He can't do that while I am still living there, can he?
Yes, he can. It is, after all, his property. This does not mean that you are without rights. First of all, your landlord will need to give you reasonable notice before he or his realtor shows the house to anyone (twenty-four hours is appropriate). Also, whoever buys the house will have to honor your lease. You can continue to live there until the lease term ends. You should also make sure that your landlord transfers your security deposit to the new owner. Get it in writing that he did so.

My roommate just moved out without paying rent this month. Who is responsible?
It all depends upon the lease or rental agreement. If both of your names are on the contract, then your ex-roommate is solely responsible to your landlord for her rent. If your name alone appears on the agreement, get ready for a rude awakening. You alone are responsible for the entire rent.

Can I sublease my apartment?
You can, unless your lease forbids it. Remember, though, that if you do, it is your name that is on the lease, not the new tenant's. If she fails to pay rent, you alone are liable to your landlord for rent. If you want out of this responsibility, you need to "assign" the contract to the new tenant. In that case, her name will go on the lease instead of yours, and all future liability will be hers alone.

My lease is about to expire. What happens if I don't move?
There are two possibilities. First, your landlord can accept rent from you, in which case you would have a new month-to-month agreement. Second, he can reject your offer of rent and evict you.

Do I need a lawyer to defend me in my eviction lawsuit?
It is almost always better to have a lawyer defend you in such situations. The real question is, can you afford one? If you think you are being evicted without justification and you want to stay in the unit, it may be worth your money to hire an attorney. If you know that your landlord has just cause to evict you, in which case he will likely win, don't waste your money.

LANDLORD RIGHTS, DUTIES, AND SOLUTIONS

Is there a limit as to what I can charge for rent?
Unless you are restricted by a local rent-control ordinance, the only limit is what the market will bear.

Can I pass on the responsibility to maintain and repair the premises to my tenant in the lease?
If your unit is a residential one, the answer is no; if it is commercial, you probably can. Remember that the warranty of habitability is implied. That means it is in every rental agreement, whether or not the agreement says so. In many states, it is illegal to try to transfer this duty to a residential tenant. In contrast, most states allow a commercial landlord to pass on this responsibility to a business tenant. The reason is that the law assumes (rightly or wrongly) that business leases are negotiated by equal parties, whereas residential landlords are usually considered to have the upper hand.

Can I increase the amount of the security deposit after the tenant has lived in the unit for some time?
Once again, it depends upon the type of agreement you have. Month-to-month tenancies can be altered on thirty days' notice. Since security deposits are a function of rent, they can be increased, but only if rent has been increased, and only if proper notice has been given. If your tenant has a lease, the security deposit can be increased only after the lease is up, *and if* you decide to renew it and charge more rent.

Can I get in trouble if I continue to use a lease form that I know contains several illegal provisions?
If the contract contains too many questionable or illegal provisions, a court may decide to void the entire agreement. In especially egregious situations, aggressive state's attorneys have been known to prosecute landlords who blatantly break the law. It is probably altogether wiser just to get a new form.

Do I have a right to object to the roommate my tenant wants to bring in?
What does the lease or rental agreement say? If the agreement limits the number of tenants or otherwise requires your permission, then, yes, he does need your permission. The impor-

tant thing as far as you are concerned is whether this person would make a good tenant. Interview and investigate him just as you would any new tenant, but do not unreasonably withhold your approval. If you do agree to let him in, be sure to add his name to the present agreement and have him sign it.

Am I liable for the acts of my apartment manager?
You most certainly are. Your manager is your "agent." As your agent, most illegal acts that she performs will be attributable to you as long as she was acting within "the course and scope" of her assigned duties. This means that you could be financially responsible for such things as acts of negligence that cause injury, acts of discrimination, or theft. Because of this, it is imperative that you hire highly qualified help.

My tenant refuses to pay his utility bills and I am forced to pay them. Can't I have them turned off?
Shutting off utilities or causing them to be shut off is usually an illegal form of "self-help." If, however, your agreement with your tenant requires your tenant to pay these bills and he does not, there is certainly nothing illegal about allowing them to be shut off.

TERMINATING THE TENANCY

My landlord wants to deduct the cost of new paint from my security deposit. Can he do that?
Probably not. If the paint is simply old, that constitutes normal wear and tear and is your landlord's responsibility, not yours. On the other hand, if you painted a room purple, then that is not normal wear and tear and you will have to bear the cost.

After the fact I, read my lease, and it says that my security deposit is nonrefundable. Is that legal?
No. Security deposits are just that—deposits. If you comply

with all the terms of the agreement and leave the place in good condition, you should get most, if not all, of your money back. If you do not, take your landlord to small claims court.

I just signed a lease with a new tenant and my old tenant refuses to leave! What can I do?
First, you must evict the old tenant. That means hiring an eviction attorney or service and paying the necessary fees and costs. You also face potential liability with the new tenant since you are required to deliver possession of the rental unit to him on time. In order to avoid this problem in the future, insert a clause into your standard lease that states something like "Occupancy is expressly contingent upon the present tenant vacating the unit." That way, if this happens again, the new tenant cannot sue you.

LAWSUITS

My tenant is suing me in superior court. I know I did nothing wrong. Do I have to defend the suit?
You really have no choice but to defend the suit. If you do not, your tenant will win by default. So, the very first thing you must do is to hire competent legal counsel. Having to defend a lawsuit when you feel you are without blame is a terrible thing since it is very expensive, emotionally draining, and quite time-consuming. But you have no choice.

GLOSSARY

Abandonment: The unilateral voluntary surrender or relinquishment of property. If both sides agree to the vacancy, it is called a surrender. If the tenant acts unilaterally, it is called an abandonment.

Answer: A written response to a lawsuit whereby the defendant denies the assertions made in the complaint. It also sets forth the grounds of the defense.

Assignment: A transfer of an agreement that permits a new party to assume completely the rights and responsibilities of the original party.

Bar Association: An association of lawyers found on local, state, and national levels.

Breach: The breaking or violating of a law, right, obligation, duty, or contract.

Burden of Proof: The duty to prove a fact in dispute. For example, in a criminal case, the burden of proof is on the government to prove guilt beyond a reasonable doubt.

Complaint: The papers that initiate a lawsuit. A complaint sets forth the parties, the jurisdiction of the court, and the grounds upon which the suit is based, and requests that the court solve the problem by granting relief.

Comprehensive General Liability Insurance: A type of insurance that covers the cost of defense as well as any damages the insured may have to pay as a result of a lawsuit.

Constructive Eviction: Any disturbance by the landlord of the tenant's possession of the rental whereby the premises are rendered unfit or unsuitable for occupancy. This allows the tenant to surrender the unit without repercussion.

Contingency Contract: A fee arrangement in which the attorney is paid only from the proceeds of a successful lawsuit. Typically, a contingency fee is anywhere from 33 to 40 percent of any money received.

Continuance: The postponement of a hearing or trial to a subsequent day or time.

Contract: An agreement between two or more parties based upon an offer, acceptance of that offer, and an exchange of money, goods, or services. A contract creates an obligation by both parties to do or not do a certain thing.

Damages: Financial compensation awarded to a person who was injured by another.

Default: Failure to answer. When a party who is being sued fails to respond to the complaint, he is in default. A party who defaults may lose the case.

Defendant: The party who is sued.

Demurrer: A motion filed by a defendant that states that the complaint against him is legally lacking.

Deposit: The delivery of money that is entrusted to another. The person receiving the money is legally bound to keep it, preserve it, and return it, unless there is legal justification to retain it.

Discovery: The pretrial process of discovering what the other party knows about the facts of the case.

Discrimination: Unfair treatment or the denial of normal privileges based upon race, creed, color, age, sex, physical ability, nationality, or religion.

Duty: A legal obligation to conform to a particular standard of conduct. Landlords usually have a duty to behave as a reasonable person would under the same or similar circumstances.

Eviction: The legal process a landlord must go through to deprive a tenant possession of the landlord's property.

Evidence: The use of witnesses, documents, records, or exhibits to prove a fact at trial.

Fee: A fixed charge for a service rendered. As opposed to a deposit, a fee is nonrefundable.

Fixed-term Agreement: A contract that gives a tenant exclusive possession of the landlord's property for a set amount of time, usually a year or more. Also known as a lease.

Fixture: Personal property that has been attached to real estate in a permanent manner so that it loses its status as personal property and becomes part of the real estate. Fixtures cannot be removed when a tenant moves.

Forcible Entry and Detainer: An expedited legal process for returning possession of land to the owner. Another term for an eviction proceeding.

Good Cause: A reason based upon substance.

Habitable: Suitable for living. It is a unit that is free of serious defects that would adversely affect health or safety.

Hold-over Tenant: A tenant who retains possession of a rental unit after the lease or month-to-month agreement has been terminated.

Implied Covenant of Quiet Enjoyment: A promise implied in every residential rental agreement that a tenant has a right to use and enjoy the property without interference.

Implied Warranty of Habitability: A promise implied in every residential rental agreement that a landlord has a duty to keep the unit in livable condition.

Judgment: The official and final decision of a court.

Jurisdiction: The geographical location of a court. A jurisdiction could be a city or a state. It also sometimes refers to the power and authority of a court to decide certain cases.

Landlord: The owner of real estate who rents property to another.

Last Month's Rent: When a tenant moves into a rental unit, it is money paid that must be applied to rent for the last month the tenant is to live in the unit.

Lease: A contract that gives a tenant exclusive possession of the landlord's property for a set amount of time, usually a year or more. Also known as a fixed-term agreement.

Liability: Penalty for failure to act in a manner as prescribed by law.

Litigation: The adversarial legal process whereby one party sues another to right an alleged wrong.

Lockout: The act by a landlord whereby the tenant is immediately put out of possession of the unit, usually accomplished by changing the locks in the tenant's absence. Lockouts are illegal.

Mitigation of Damages: The duty of an injured party to exercise reasonable diligence to minimize his damage. In landlord-tenant law, it is the requirement put upon a landlord to re-let his unit as soon as it is feasible to do so after a tenant has illegally moved out.

Month-to-Month Agreement: A rental arrangement that can continue indefinitely but can be terminated or otherwise changed on thirty days' notice.

Motion: A request made before a court that asks the court to rule on a matter in a certain way.

Motion to Quash: A motion that seeks to throw out a lawsuit because the defendant was improperly served.

Negligence: The failure to do something that a reasonable person would have done, or taking an action that a reasonable person would not have taken.

Notice: Informing someone of a necessary fact. Depending upon the circumstances, a person can be said to have notice if he actually knows of the fact or should know of it.

Notice to Pay Rent or Quit: A written notice given by a land-lord to his tenant that states that the landlord intends to repossess the property if rent is not paid in full in a specific number of days.

Notice to Perform Covenant or Quit: A written notice given by a landlord to his tenant that states that the landlord intends to repossess the property if the tenant fails to take certain actions in a specific number of days.

Nuisance: The unreasonable, unwarranted, or unlawful use by a person of his property that interferes with another's use and enjoyment of his property.

Paralegal: A person who has some knowledge of the law, but is not a lawyer and cannot give legal advice.

Party/Parties: The people involved in a lawsuit. Each person or entity is a party to the suit; collectively, all plaintiffs and defendants are the parties.

Plaintiff: The person who initiates a lawsuit by filing the complaint.

Privacy: The right to be let alone.

Quiet Enjoyment: The right to use and enjoy property in peace and without disturbance.

Remedies: Options that the law offers to redress a wrong.

Rent: Money paid (or sometimes services rendered) for use and occupation of property.

Rent Abatement: Rent withholding. A remedy option for tenants whereby they withhold all or part of their rent in response to a violation of the law by their landlord.

Rental Agreement: An agreement between a landlord and a tenant that sets forth the terms of the tenancy. Most rental agreements create a month-to-month tenancy.

Rent Control: Laws enacted on a city-by-city basis that dictate the amount of rent landlords can charge tenants.

Rent Strike: An organized undertaking by tenants in which rent is withheld until grievances between the landlord and tenants are resolved.

Repair and Deduct: A legal remedy that permits a tenant to deduct a portion of her rent to pay for repairs that the landlord has refused to make.

Retainer: Money paid to an attorney that creates an attorney-client relationship.

Retaliatory Rent Increase: An illegal rent increase imposed by a landlord because a tenant utilized a legal remedy that the landlord did not like.

Security Deposit: Money deposited by the tenant with the landlord to ensure performance by the tenant of the terms of the agreement. It is refundable unless the tenant fails to pay rent, harms the premises, or otherwise violates the terms of the agreement.

Self-help: Taking the law into one's own hands without following legal procedure.

Serve/Service: The delivery of a legal document upon a party.

Small Claims Court: A special court that provides informal, quick, and inexpensive resolution of small matters. The limit is usually under $5,000, although it varies from state to state.

Sublease: An agreement between an old tenant and a new tenant whereby the new tenant agrees to move into the unit and pay the rent. The old tenant remains liable should the new tenant fail to live up to the rental agreement with the landlord.

Sue: To commence a legal proceeding.

Summons: The legal instrument initiating a lawsuit. Delivered to the defendant with a complaint, it notifies the defendant of the suit.

Superior Court: The court where disagreements over substantial sums of money are resolved. Sometimes also known as municipal, county, or district court.

Surrender: The giving up of property before the term is over. If both sides agree to the vacancy, it is called a surrender. If the tenant acts unilaterally, it is called an abandonment.

Tenancy: The period of a tenant's possession of the property. It can be either for a fixed amount of time, usually a year or more, or for a shorter period, usually month-to-month.

Tenant: One who rents and pays for property.

Terminate: Legally ending a rental agreement.

Tort: A private or civil wrong or injury caused by another.

Trespass: The unlawful interference with another's property rights. A landlord can trespass on his own property if he has rented it to someone else.

Unconscionable: An agreement that is so one-sided as to oppress one of the parties. If found unconscionable, a court will throw out the objectionable clause or contract. Courts look to the relative sophistication of both parties when making this determination.

Unlawful Detainer: An expedited legal process for returning possession of land to the owner. Another term for an eviction proceeding.

Vacate and Sue: A remedy sometimes available to tenants that allows them to end a lease early, move out, and sue their landlord.

Void: Null; ineffectual; having no legal force or effect.

Waive/Waiver: Knowingly giving up some right.

Waste: Abusing, destroying, or allowing property to fall into disrepair.

Wear and Tear: Ordinary and reasonable use.

INDEX